Something to Think About

A Collection of Bright Spots,
BIG Things, and Good Stuff
for Your Soul

James M. Wells

Something to Think About

All rights reserved. This book or any portion thereof may not be reproduced or used without the express written permission of the author except for the use of brief quotations in a book review or noncommercial uses as permitted by copyright law.

This is a collection of stories to illustrate specific points. Many are actual events, retold subject to the limitations of memory. In protect the reputations of the innocent (and the occasionally guilty), while remaining true to the nature of the events, identifying characteristics and details such as physical properties, occupations, etc. may have been changed

ISBN (Paperback Edition): ISBN: 979-8-9858607-2-6

Evensong Press
An Imprint of Lonesome Pine Creative Arts, LLC
P.O. 3612 Wise, Virginia 24293
www.evensongbooks.com

Cover Design, Book Design and Production
Lonesome Pine Creative Arts, LLC

Scripture quotations taken from
The Holy Bible, New International Version® NIV
Except where otherwise noted.
Copyright © 1973 1978 1984 2011 by Biblica, Inc.™
Used by permission. All rights reserved worldwide.

All Stories, Essays, Poems and Big Ideas
Copyright © James M. Wells
Used by Permission

Something to Think About, First Edition
Copyright © 2022 Evensong Press

In memory

My first Professor of Homiletics, Ainsworth Chapman, Eastern Christian College, Bel Air, MD.

Dedicated to

Eddie Callahan, who mentored me into the Preaching Ministry.

Dr. David Enyart, retired Professor of Pastoral Ministries, Johnson University, Knoxville, TN, my second Professor of Homiletics.

Sincere thanks to

My patient and persevering wife, Karen

My children and grandchildren

Johnny and Joyce Wells and sisters

The gracious souls of Norton Christian Church

The excellent staff and students of EduCare Preschool

The semi-illustrious Bardstown Brothers, my cohort of Christian encouragement

WNVA, WAXM, WLSD, WDIC

Sandy Wardell

Jim Wardell, Renaissance man

Table of Contents

Introduction 1
Author's Note 2

Part I
Bright Spots

Do You Need Church? 5
Wise Words from Ward Cleaver 6
The Best Laid Plans 8
And Then Jonah Puked 10
Hell Can Wait 12
The One about Tony, Tony 14
Someone Shot an Arrow into the Air 16
The Jerk Who Went to Church 18
Arranging Your Life 20
The Company You Keep 21
From the Mouth of a Babe 22
Speeding Up to Slow Down? 23
Born OK the First Time? 24
The Best Place We've Never Been 26
Wanting to Go Home 27
What Will Heaven Be Like? 28
The One about Roxie the Dog 29
When Bad Things Come My Way 30
Making a Difference 32
The Grumpy Monk 34
Fitting In 36

Is IT Missing In Your Life?... 37
Is God Trustworthy? 38
Praise Be to God for His Mysterious Ways.................... 39
No Homework in Heaven 40
What a Sweet Little Girl.. 41
I Like Mommy Better 42
Buzzard Bait 43
Fighting the Devil... 44
A Manly Man 45
Words of Wisdom.. 46
Paris Can Wait.. 47
A Little Boy's Confession 48
It Got Out of the Way!.. 49
Knowing Your Strengths... 50
Look What God Paid for Us...51
Spending Time with Yourself 52
Being the Church To the Church.................................. 53
Rationalizing Sin 54
Get Out!" 56
The Rock 57
On Being the Chosen Ones 58
No Other Name 59
Watching Two Games at Once 60
Cheer for the Church! 62
Faith Always Trusts.. 64
Just Say the Word, Lord. 65
You Are Not Going to Believe This............................... 66
Holy Hypocrisy, Batman! 68
Hatin' Life? 69

How Long Will She Be in Heaven..................................70
The Right Car at the Right Time..................................71
The Iceberg Metaphor..72
A Great Question to Think About.................................74
The Unholy Car..75
"He Did That for Us?"..76
The Perfect Name for a Cemetery.................................77
What a Way to Put It...78
The Best Thanksgiving Answer.....................................80
Are You Thankful for You?..81
When Jesus Showed Up..82
And It Came to Pass..83
A New Year's Prayer...84

Part II
BIG Things

BIG Things..84

PART III
Good Stuff for the Soul

Ministry Moments...123
Be Like Bill..124
Do You Have a Song...125
A Snake in the Grass..127
This Is the Day the LORD Has Made..........................129
Serendipitous Small Things..131
The Beast..133

Walla Walla!	134
Grace	137
I Can't Wait	138
In the Silence of the Sanctuary	140
We Are Who We Are	142
Walk with Me	143
He Who Never Began	145
The Calm in the Midst of the Strife	146
In All Things	147
Lay Your Hand Upon Me, Lord	148
In Remembrance of Me	149
The Little Red Car	150
I Wonder	152
Route 666	154
Sometimes My Shirt Tickles Me	155
Really?	157
A Lesson from Cracker Barrel	158
It Made Me an Offer I Couldn't Refuse	160
Bird Watching	161
Bob's Gulf Station	164
Oh My, How Time Goes By	166
Making an Impression	169
We are the Church. . . And We Win!	171
The Fringe of Fellowship	173
It Is On The Way!	176
God Smiled	178
Breakfast with Jesus	180
The Continuity of Communion	185
A Tale of Two Churches	188

Boga. Boga	189
God Allows U-Turns	191
The Greatest Question Ever Asked	192
I Can Still Hear the Laughter	194
A Poem of Praise	195
The Christmas Story (more or less)	196
The Fullness of Time	198
He Came into the World	200
'Twas The Week Before Christmas	202
A Reminder That I Was A Grandad	204
A Story	205
My Sheep is Safe!	212
Tough as Nails	213
A Breakthrough	215
A Note on a Tree	217
About the Author	221
Books By This Author	222

Something to Think About

Blessed is the man who does not walk in the counsel of the wicked or stand in the way of sinners or sit in the seat of mockers.

But his delight is in the law of the LORD and on his law he meditates day and night.

He is like a tree planted by streams of water, which yields its fruit in season and whose leaf does not wither. Whatever he does prospers.

Not so the wicked! They are like chaff that the wind blows away.

Therefore the wicked will not stand in the judgment, nor sinners in the assembly of the righteous.

For the LORD watches over the way of the righteous, but the way of the wicked will perish.

Psalm 1
New International Version

Introduction

"Something to think about, and that's today's Bright Spot from Norton Christian Church."

Those words, or similar words, have aired over 40,000 times on radio stations in Southwest Virginia where Pastor James Wells has served Norton Christian Church since 1984.

Known as "Bright Spots," the 60-second broadcasts are designed to present a positive Christian message, offer encouragement to those who may be discouraged, and illustrate Biblical Truths in a way that are entertaining, often humorous, and always thought-provoking.

Many of the "Spots" are clearly Biblically based and are humorous, but some are serious and may require a little extra effort to find "Bright Spot" that is the presence of God in all things. As Jesus says, "He who has ears, let him hear."

Each Bright Spot is coupled with related Bible verses to contemplate as the reader reflects on the story and how it relates to their own life and spiritual journey.

In addition to "Bright Spots," you will find a section called *BIG Things*. These are one or two sentence sermon summaries, often called

The Big Idea, or *The Main Thing* by other preachers and teachers. In the study of Homiletics, it called a "thesis statement."

This book includes two hundred "BIG Things" meant to encourage the meditation of Biblical truths and serve as inspiration for teachers and preachers as they prepare their own sermons and lessons

The book concludes with a collection of 50 longer original stories and poems that reflect on a family, faith, and what it means to be a Christian.

Author's Note

Since my first year of Bible College in 1975, I have collected and written thousands of stories. I try to abide by the Shakespearean dictum, "brevity is the soul of wit," but I do not always succeed.

I pray and hope that time spent in this book may, indeed, give you "something to think about," and bless you in your spiritual formation in Christ Jesus.

James M. Wells
Wise, VA
January, 2022

Part I
Bright Spots

Do You Need Church?

Six o'clock one Sunday morning, a girl from our church went into her into her parent's bedroom and announced impatiently, "It's morning o'clock."

Hoping to get a few extra minutes in bed, Mommy asked her to lie back down, telling the little girl that it was "still sleepy time."

But the little girl had other ideas and persisted in her attempt to rouse her Mommy. "Mommy," she proclaimed, louder than at first. "Mommy. Mom-Mom-Mommmmmy!"

Muffled by the covers, the exhausted young mother tried to explain, "It is STILL bedtime Honey. What is so important?"

The little girl replied, "Mommy. I need Church this morning."

I love the way kids see and say things.

* * *

Let us consider how to stir up one another to love and good works, not neglecting to meet together, as is the habit of some, but encouraging one another.

Hebrews 10: 24,25

Wise Words from Ward Cleaver

When I was growing up, one of my favorite TV shows was "Leave it to Beaver."

It still is.

I recall an episode in which Ward was explaining to Wally and the Beaver about having to do things they did not want to do.

In this case they needed to do something for their mother.

Ward told the boys, "Sometimes you have to make yourself a little *unhappy* to make someone else *happy*."

There is an excellent theological point about love to be learned from what he said. The Bible word for that kind of love is "agape."

It is the kind of love God has for us. The Cross is proof of that. It is the kind of love we are to have for each other, a love that is selfless and sacrificial.

Ward Cleaver was right, sometimes we need to be willing to make ourselves a little unhappy, to make the people we love happier.

We seldom hear that kind of counsel on television today, but it is a message well worth receiving.

* * *

If I speak in the tongues of men or of angels, but do not have love, I am only a resounding gong or a clanging cymbal.

If I have the gift of prophecy and can fathom all mysteries and all knowledge, and if I have a faith that can move mountains, but do not have love, I am nothing.

If I give all I possess to the poor and give over my body to hardship that I may boast, but do not have love, I gain nothing.

Love is patient, love is kind. It does not envy, it does not boast, it is not proud.

It does not dishonor others, it is not self-seeking, it is not easily angered, it keeps no record of wrongs.

Love does not delight in evil but rejoices with the truth.

It always protects, always trusts, always hopes, always perseveres.

Love never fails.

1 Corinthians 13:1-8

The Best Laid Plans

In 1785, the famous Scottish poet Robert Burns wrote, "the best laid plans of mice and men often go awry.

This commentary on how often our plans fall through is as relevant today as it ever was. You may have heard it said, "If you want to make God laugh, tell Him your plans."

I was reminded of this while vacationing at Myrtle Beach several years ago.

My wife and I talked with a young man from Bulgaria and asked how he came to the states. He told us that back in Bulgaria he had a girlfriend, and she moved to the States, and after a bit of time she convinced him to move too. So he did.

Then his girlfriend broke up with him.

By the time my wife and I met this young man, he had a new girlfriend. She lived in Bulgaria and wanted him to move back there. It would be interesting to know how those plans turned out, and did God chuckle?

What plans have you made lately?

* * *

Trust in the Lord with all your heart and lean not on your own understanding; in all ways submit to Him, and He make your paths straight.

Proverbs 3:5-6

* * *

In their hearts, humans plan their course, but the Lord establishes their steps.

Proverbs 16:9

* * *

Now listen, you who say, "Today or tomorrow we will go to this or that city, spend a year there, carry on business and make money."

Why, you do not even know what will happen tomorrow. Instead, you ought to say, "If it is the Lord's will, we will live and do this or that.

James 4:13-25

And Then Jonah Puked

One of the ministries of Norton Christian Church is the EduCare Preschool program that serves children between the ages of three and five. Throughout the school year, I will visit the children to conduct Bible Story Time.

Just before graduation one year, I visited to review a few of the Bible Stories I had shared with the students.

When it comes to telling the kids Bible stories, I always do what Andy Griffith did when he told the story of the founding of America.

I add "a little jam to the biscuits."

Sometimes more than others.

As it turns out, the kids do that, too.

For example, during this visit when we reviewed the story of Jonah, we talked about how "nasty, smelly, slimly, gross and disgusting" it was in the belly of that great fish and how Jonah was in there for three days and nights.

I asked what God caused the Great Fish to do to deliver Jonah, and all the kids, as expected, made vomiting sounds.

Then I asked, "What did Jonah do after the fish threw him up onto the shore?"

Without hesitation, one little girl replied, "Puked."

I love the way kids see things and say things.

* * *

"Those who cling to worthless idols turn away from God's love for them. But I, with shouts of grateful praise, will sacrifice to you.

What I have vowed I will make good. I will say, 'Salvation comes from the Lord.'"

Jonah 2:8,9

* * *

"Truly I tell you, unless you change and become like little children, you will never enter the kingdom of heaven. Therefore, whoever takes the lowly position of this child is the greatest in the kingdom of heaven. And whoever welcomes one such child in my name welcomes me."

Matthew 18:3-5

Hell Can Wait

I was driving up the interstate to Louisville, KY. A casket company truck passed me. On the back of the trailer there was a sign which read, "Please drive carefully—heaven can wait."

Now the first thing that came to my mind was, "What about hell?"

Why is it that most people seem to think everybody is heading to heaven?

Why do we hear so little about hell?

Perhaps it is because there are those who believe that the doctrine of hell is inconsistent with a loving God. This is built on the false assumption that the supreme attribute of God is love.

It is not. It is holiness.

His love for us is a manifestation of His holiness, and His desire for us to be holy is a manifestation of that love.

We cannot ignore that the same Book that teaches us about heaven teaches us about hell, too. We cannot pick and choose which doctrines to believe teach and preach.

Fortunately, there is more to the story.

In the Book of Acts we read that through repentance and baptism we are forgiven and with that promise in mind, we know that hell can wait.

Forever.

* * *

"Repent and be baptized, every one of you, in the name of Jesus Christ for the forgiveness of your sins. And you will receive the gift of the Holy Spirit. The promise is for you and your children and for all who are far off—for all whom the Lord our God will call."

Acts 2:38,39

* * *

For God so loved the world that he gave his one and only Son, that whoever believes in him shall not perish but have eternal life. For God did not send his Son into the world to condemn the world, but to save the world through him. Whoever believes in him is not condemned, but whoever does not believe stands condemned already because they have not believed in the name of God's one and only Son.

John 3:16-18

The One about Tony, Tony

While on my annual "Retreat of the Soul" with my fellow Bardstown Brothers, we had the opportunity to have lunch with a Catholic priest named Gary.

We enjoyed getting to know each other. Gary told us a story about a parishioner who came to him about a lost item.

Gary asked if she had appealed to St. Anthony. In Catholicism, St. Anthony is the patron saint of lost things. Then Gary proceeded to tell us a clever prayer that some offer to St. Anthony when they need to find something.

"Tony, Tony come around. Something's lost and must be found."

The whole table erupted with laughter, not only because it was funny in the ways we usually think of jokes, but because it was unexpected.

You never know when, where, or with whom you will find an opportunity to share in the gift of humor; to enjoy a time to laugh.

* * *

A cheerful heart is good medicine, but a crushed spirit dries up the bones.

Proverbs 17:22

* * *

Our mouths were filled with laughter, our tongues with songs of joy. Then it was said among the nations, "The Lord has done great things for them."

The Lord has done great things for us, and we are filled with joy.

Psalm 126:2,3

* * *

There is a time for everything, and a season for every activity under the heavens: a time to be born and a time to die, a time to plant and a time to uproot, a time to kill and a time to heal, a time to tear down and a time to build, a time to weep and a time to laugh, a time to mourn and a time to dance.

Ecclesiastes 3:1-4

Someone Shot
an Arrow into the Air

And it landed in my backyard.

One day, several years ago, I was mowing my grass and I saw an arrow sticking out of the ground. Someone, at some time, had taken aim at something and missed. I have kept that arrow in my study ever since as a reminder of sin.

The word "sin," and its various forms, is used found 656 times in the Bible. The one that paints the best picture is the New Testament word meaning "to miss the mark," like shooting an arrow and missing the target.

We all know what it is to miss the mark, to set our sights on a target only to find afterward that our follow-through did not achieve what we intended. Even in our spiritual goals.

Not everyone believes in the reality of sin. Satan has deceived many souls. Just as he did in the Garden of Gethsemane, he calls into question the credibility and authority of God's Word.

He leads people to believe that things are "mistakes" or "life choices," but not "sins." That everything is relative.

But the Bible makes it clear that the absolute truth is that the entire human race has missed the mark when it comes to our own holiness and our own feeble attempts to justify ourselves. We have all sinned.

Only once we have accepted that fundamental truth, can we embrace Good News of Christ Jesus who "came into the world to save sinners (**1 Timothy 1:15**).

* * *

All have sinned and fall short of the glory of God, and all are justified freely by his grace through the redemption that came by Christ Jesus. God presented Christ as a sacrifice of atonement, through the shedding of his blood—to be received by faith.

Romans 3:23-25

* * *

God demonstrates his own love for us in this: While we were still sinners, Christ died for us.

Romans 5:8

The Jerk Who Went to Church

Many churches practice what is called "the passing of the peace."

At a church in the Pacific Northwest, during the morning worship service, the time came for "the passing of the peace," and everyone stood and greeted each other in the name of Jesus, saying "peace be with you."

Later in the week the pastor received a letter of complaint from one of the church's new members, a lawyer, who said, "I am writing to complain about the congregational practice known as the passing of the peace. I disagree with it both personally and professionally, and I am prepared to take legal action to stop it."

The pastor phoned the man and asked why, and he was told, "It is an invasion of my privacy."

I told my kids as they were growing up: The jerks will be with you always. Just don't be one.

That is good advice for adults too.

* * *

In everything, do to others what you would have them do to you, for this sums up the Law and the Prophets.

Matthew 7:12

* * *

Do not repay anyone evil for evil. Be careful to do what is right in the eyes of everyone. If it is possible, as far as it depends on you, live at peace with everyone. Do not take revenge, my dear friends, but leave room for God's wrath, for it is written: "It is mine to avenge; I will repay," says the Lord.

Do not be overcome by evil but overcome evil with good.

Romans 12:17-19, 21

* * *

"You have heard that it was said, 'Love your neighbor and hate your enemy.' But I tell you, love your enemies and pray for those who persecute you, that you may be children of your Father in heaven."

Matthew 5:43-45

Arranging Your Life

A man bought one of Whistler's paintings and asked the great artist to assist him in finding the right place for it in his home. The artist agreed to help and waited patiently while the man held the painting in various locations.

No place seemed exactly right.

Finally, Whistler said, "You are going about this all wrong. What you need to do is to move all the furniture out of the house, hang the painting where you want it, and then arrange the furniture around the painting."

Do you need to rearrange things in your life? Do you struggle to bring the pieces together; to get your priorities in order?

If so, you need to move everything out, invite God in, and then arrange everything else around Him.

* * *

Seek first the kingdom of God and his righteousness, and all these things will be added to you.

Matthew 6:3

The Company You Keep

A Sunday School teacher asked her class of young boys, "How many of you want to go to heaven?"

Every hand, of course, shot up, but one. The teacher asked, "Charlie, you mean you do not want to go to heaven?"

Charlie replied, "Sure I want to go to heaven, but not with this bunch."

Sometimes, even children can be judgmental.

Just a cute story to brighten your day.

* * *

You are the light of the world.

A city set on a hill cannot be hidden. Nor do people light a lamp and put it under a basket, but on a stand, and it gives light to all in the house.

In the same way, let your light shine before others, so that they may see your good works and give glory to your Father who is in heaven.

Matthew 5:14-16

From the Mouth of a Babe

It is Father's Day and souls are coming together for our 11:00 Worship Hour as he walks in holding his daddy's hand.

He is just three-and-a-half years old, with reddish hair, and a contagious smile, and wearing a brown ball cap. He seldom displays any evidence of shyness.

He looks up at me and exclaims, "I am so excited about church today!"

Yes, Jacob loves Sunday Morning Church!

I am sure that is what David had in mind when he sang, "I was glad when they said to me, 'Let us go to the house of the LORD.'"

Psalm 122:1

* * *

"Praise the LORD. I will extol the LORD with all my heart in the council of the upright and in the assembly."

Psalm 111:1

Speeding Up to Slow Down?

I have been thinking about the way technology seems to push us along faster and faster; spur us on to do more and more.

We use busy-ness as a substitute for real productivity, and technology feeds into this. Even when we relax, we do so in a rush. There are even options to allow us to speed up streaming videos we watch for entertainment.

Not long ago, driving home from Kingsport, TN, I heard an interesting statistic on the radio: Seventy percent of people prefer to take a book or a magazine with them when they fly. Not a laptop or some new technology, but a book or a magazine.

Why? Can it be they are trying to escape for a few hours, and return to simpler things?

This is something to think about: We have to sit in a tube with wings, ascend to 30,000 feet and zip along at 500 miles an hour to find a chance to slow down.

* * *

Be still and know that I am God; I will be exalted among the nations, I will be exalted in the earth."

Psalm 46:10

Born OK the First Time?

You see a lot of interesting plates and bumper stickers driving down the highway. A while back I saw a bumper sticker that said, "I was born Ok the first time."

You know what that is all about don't you.

It is a cheap shot at the Biblical doctrine that all have sinned and need to be born again.

When it comes to such matters, I choose to believe The Bible, and it has a lot to say about the eternal danger of mocking sin and following one's own ways and desires.

In Psalms, David warned us that "the wicked freely strut about when what is vile is honored among men."

Psalms 12:8

It is not popular to say and it is not an easy teaching, but the Bible is clear on the differences between the ways of man and the way of God.

We were not born OK the first time, but there is a Bright Spot: Jesus died and came back to life so that we can be *born again*.

* * *

There is a way that seems right to a man, but in the end, it leads to death.

Proverbs 14:12

* * *

Here is a trustworthy saying that deserves full acceptance: Christ Jesus came into the world to save sinners

1 Timothy 1:15

* * *

All have sinned and fall short of the glory of God.

Romans 3:23

* * *

I tell you the truth, no one can see the kingdom of God unless he is born again.

John 3:3

The Best Place We've Never Been

His name was Bob. A kind, gentle man. A WWII Vet. And the first person I baptized as pastor of Norton Christian Church.

In his eighties, Bob had an accident which hospitalized him. One day when I visited him I noticed a small white board on the wall next to his bed.

It had a number on it, the number 5.

I asked Bob about it and he said that is the number of days until he gets to go home. And then he paused and softly said, "Home. It's the best place I've ever been."

I never forgot those words and the way ol' Bob said them. That is the way I see heaven. Heaven is the best place we've <u>never</u> been.

But one day heaven *will be* the best place we've *ever* been. And I am sure Bob is saying that now.

***

No eye has seen, no ear has heard, no mind has conceived what God has planned for those who love him.

I Corinthians 2:9

Wanting to Go Home

During his first day of EduCare Preschool of Norton Christian Church, a little boy was having separation anxiety. He cried a lot and was afraid

The Preschool Director took him into her office and held him. She hugged him and rocked him. She reassured him that everything was going to be all right and his mommy would be back soon.

Then she asked, "How can I help you?"

He, still weeping, replied, "I'm. . . just. . . trying to find. . . my way back. . . home."

Do you ever feel that way. God knows and understands.

*　*　*

Do not let your hearts be troubled. Trust in God; trust also in me.

In my Father's house are many rooms; if it were not so, I would have told you. I am going there to prepare a place for you. And if I go and prepare a place for you, I will come back and take you to be with me that you also may be where I am.

John 14:1-3

What Will Heaven Be Like?

Many preachers and teachers have research assistants who help them prepare by gathering material and information.

I have the Little Theologians of EduCare Preschool.

In preparing a message about Heaven, I asked our four- and five year-olds students what they thought Heaven will be like. As you can imagine, I received some great answers:

- Heaven is like you are having fun.
- It will be agreeable (*and polite, I think*).
- It is about love.
- There will be apples and bananas.
- There will be clowns" (*I hope not*).
- God is going to tell us stories. (*I hope so*).

The one that summed it all up for me was when a little boy said rather matter-of-factly:

"Better than this place."

The One about Roxie the Dog

Several years ago I was speaking with a man named Robert who told me the story about his young grandson Jamie and Jamie's dog named Roxie.

Jamie was getting ready for Church on Easter Sunday, and he had his Bible opened on his bed. Roxie jumped up and began to eat the Bible, devouring several pages.

Jamie later commented by saying, "And it did not do her any good. She is still as mean as ever."

* * *

I have hidden your word in my heart that I might not sin against you.

Psalm 119:11

* * *

Therefore everyone who hears these words of mine and puts them into practice is like a wise man who built his house on the rock. The rain came down, the streams rose, and the winds blew and beat against that house; yet it did not fall, because it had its foundation on the rock.

Matthew 7:24-27

When Bad Things Come My Way

Contrary to what many believe, the call to follow Jesus is a call to difficult times and challenging situations. Jesus himself tells us this and calls for us to put our faith in him.

And so when trouble comes, we have a choice to make. We can give up and give in to our own understanding or we can trust that God has a plan for us.

I've written this poem to summarize my thoughts and remind me of what is important when bad things come my way:

* * *

When Bad Things Come My Way

When bad things come my way in life,
for reasons I do not know,
I choose to keep on trusting God,
so in His grace to grow.

When bad things come my way in life,
I will not stop believing,
that God is up to something good;
there are blessings worth receiving.

* * *

In this world you will have trouble but take heart! I have overcome the world.

John 16:33

* * *

Consider it pure joy, my brothers, whenever you face trials of many kinds, because you know that the testing of your faith develops perseverance.

James 1:2-3

* * *

To keep me from becoming conceited because of these surpassingly great revelations, there was given me a thorn in my flesh, a messenger of Satan, to torment me.

Three times I pleaded with the Lord to take it away from me. But he said to me, 'My grace is sufficient for you, for my power is made perfect in weakness.'

Therefore I will boast all the more gladly about my weaknesses, so that Christ's power may rest on me.

That is why, for Christ's sake, I delight in weaknesses, in insults, in hardships, in persecutions, in difficulties. For when I am weak, then I am strong.

II Corinthians 12:7-10

Making a Difference

In the movie, *It's a Wonderful Life*, by Frank Capra, Jimmy Stewart played George Bailey, who lived in a small town called Bedford Falls.

In one scene, Violet Bick is planning to leave Bedford Falls, and she goes to George for advice and help.

George gives her some money and words of encouragement, and she kisses him on the cheek and says, "I'm glad I know you George Bailey."

George Bailey made a difference, but he did not realize what a difference he made in the lives of the people of Bedford Falls until later in the movie.

I'll avoid any spoilers here, but I suspect most people know the rest of that story.

Look for ways for God to use you to be a George Bailey to others. You just never know what God can do through you.

* * *

The joy of the LORD is your strength.

Nehemiah 8:10

* * *

You are the salt of the earth. But if the salt loses its saltiness, how can it be made salty again?

It is no longer good for anything, except to be thrown out and trampled by men.

You are the light of the world. A city on a hill cannot be hidden.

Neither do people light a lamp and put it under a bowl. Instead they put it on its stand, and it gives light to everyone in the house.

In the same way, let your light shine before men, that they may see your good deeds and praise your Father in heaven.

Matthew 5:13-16

The Grumpy Monk

In Myrtle Beach, SC, there are countless restaurants. Karen and I drove by one named *The Grumpy Monk*. We did not visit that one, but maybe the next time.

I was fascinated by that name. I was so curious as to the origin, that I contacted The restaurant and was told the name comes from a nickname one of the owners had in college.

I am sure there is an interesting story behind that, but here is the fun part: I actually met a grumpy monk!

Best of all, he was the monk designated to be the greeter in monastery's visitor's center. My fellow Bardstown Brothers often joke about the night we met the grumpy monk.

We all have moods we go through.

My wife Karen assures me that I can be as grouchy and grumpy as the best of them.

It could be that my grumpy monk was having a bad night, and the last thing he needed was to have ten protestant pastors invade his peaceful place.

Or it may be his natural temperament.

In any case, the next time you get a case of the grumpies, think about The Grumpy Monk (both of them).

* * *

Create in me a pure heart, O God, and renew a steadfast spirit within me.

Do not cast me from your presence or take your Holy Spirit from me.

Restore to me the joy of your salvation and grant me a willing spirit, to sustain me.

Psalm 51:10-12

* * *

Do everything without grumbling or arguing, so that you may become blameless and pure children of God without fault in a warped and crooked generation.

Then you will shine among them like stars in the sky as you hold firmly to the word of life. And then I will be able to boast on the day of Christ that I did not run or labor in vain

Philippians 2:14-16

Fitting In

During a prayer meeting at Norton Christian Church, I asked, "Is there a need in the Church we need to pray about?"

One mother said, "We need to pray for our young people. They face so much pressure in the world."

She then told us about her son's friend, who was going through a hard time and got into some trouble.

One evening her son said, "Mom, do you think he was just trying to fit it?"

She then said to all of us, "Isn't that what we all want? To fit in?"

The Church of Jesus is designed BY Jesus for everyone to fit in. While we all have different personalities, gifts and abilities, we form ONE Body in Christ.

The Church really is a place we can call home.

***

But in fact God has arranged the parts in the body, ever one of them, just as he wanted them to be."

I Corinthians 12:18

Is IT Missing In Your Life?

Several years ago Karen and I picked up a bag of small decorative rocks for our little pond beside our deck. Each stone was engraved with a word describing an attractive thought or a praiseworthy virtue.

There were 11 stones with these words: Smile. Harmony. Friends. Welcome. Peace. Love. Hope. Faith. Trust. Create. Dream.

I immediately noticed something missing. *Grace* was missing. I wondered if it could be the unique place grace has in Christianity?

There is a story about C. S. Lewis attending a conference on comparative religions. Some of the participants were debating Christianity's unique contribution among world religions.

Lewis said, "That's easy. It's grace."

Grace is a beautiful thing. And something to think about.

* * *

For it is by grace you have been saved, through faith —and this not from yourselves, it is the gift of God—not by works, so that no one can boast.

Ephesians 2:8, 9

Is God Trustworthy?

A couple of years ago there was a billboard in Duffield, VA with these words: "Trust us with your heart." It was an advertisement by the Regional Heart Center.

Think about that.

Isn't that what God says to us?

"Trust me with your heart. Trust me with your soul. Trust me with your mind. Trust me with your life. Trust me."

Is God trustworthy? You know He is.

* * *

And we know that in all things God works for the good of those who love him, who have been called according to his purpose."

Romans 8:28

* * *

And without faith it is impossible to please God, because anyone who comes to him must believe that he exists and that he rewards those who earnestly seek him.

Hebrews 11:6

Praise Be to God for His Mysterious Ways

A member of our Church Family stood in line to vote during a presidential election. There were some conversations taking place in line, and she expressed her opinion.

One of the other voters started to get a little agitated, and our Church Member said, "Well, no matter who is elected president, God is still King."

The agitated voter replied, "I don't think He has anything to do with it."

He could not be more wrong. I may not understand the mysterious ways of God, but I know and am glad He is involved in the affairs of men.

* * *

Praise be to the name of God forever and ever; wisdom and power are his. He changes times and seasons; he sets up kings and deposes them.

Daniel 2:20,21

His dominion is an eternal dominion; his kingdom endures from generation to generation.

Daniel 4:34, 35

No Homework in Heaven

I met a Christian named Janet. Janet taught a Sunday School Class.

She told me about a time a little girl in her class asked, "Will there be homework in heaven?"

Janet thought for a moment and said, "Whatever will make you happy will be in heaven."

And the little girl shouted, "Oh boy. There's no homework!"

The beauty of child-like faith.

* * *

No eye has seen, no ear has heard, no mind has conceived what God has prepared for those who love him.

I Corinthians 2:9

What a Sweet Little Girl

I walked through Educare Preschool one day during playtime. A little girl named Katie ran up to me and hugged me. She went back to a table where she was putting train tracks together and asked me to play with her.

I thanked her and said I have some work to do upstairs. When I came back down she asked me again to play with her.

I could not say no to her this time. I would have been doomed for all time. She and I and three other preschoolers worked on the train tracks.

I said to them, "you are doing better than I am at this. You are smarter than me."

To which sweet Katie replied, "It is because you are old?"

I do not think she is as sweet as I once thought.

***

Even to your old age and gray hairs I am He, I am He who will sustain you. I have made you and I will carry you; I will sustain you and I will rescue you.

Isaiah 46:4

I Like Mommy Better

My daughter, Katie, and son-in-law, Mitch, have five children.

On morning after Katie finished a refreshing morning shower and was ready to face the day, she encountered a problem with four of her kids. They were in the living room, still in their pajamas playing games on their Wii.

Mom said, "Ok kiddos, time to brush your teeth, get dressed and feed the animals."

They stared at her with blank faces, and then continued playing on the game console.

Mom clapped her hands and said "NOW!"

They finally started moving.

As she turned to walk away, Katie heard one of the kids whisper, "I like mommy better when she is asleep."

Kids. You gotta love them.

Buzzard Bait

A few years ago, a coyote died near the house where my daughter and son-in-law and my five grandkids lived.

Our grandson Eli, 8-years-old at the time, noticed buzzards circling it.

He got it in his mind that he wanted to shoot a buzzard with his slingshot, but he had a problem: How to get close enough to a buzzard... safely.

Ever the clever boy, he is he came up with a bright idea.

He used his little sister Mollie as buzzard bait.

He had her play dead while he hid with his slingshot and waited for some buzzards!

Thankfully, it didn't work.

* * *

"Let the little children come to me, and do not hinder them, for the kingdom of heaven belongs to such as these."

Matthew 19:14

Fighting the Devil

Mollie is much more than "buzzard bait."

When she was eight years old, she drew a picture of the devil and asked her mom, "Can I put this on my wall?"

Mom asked, "Why would you want to put a picture of the devil on your wall?"

Mollie said, "So I can throw stuff at it."

That was Mollie's way of fighting the good fight.

* * *

Be self-controlled and alert. Your enemy the devil prowls around like a roaring lion looking for someone to devour. Resist him, standing firm in the faith.

I Peter 5:8, 9

* * *

Finally, be strong in the Lord and in his mighty power. Put on the full armor of God so that you can take your stand against the devil's schemes.

Ephesians 6:10, 11

A Manly Man

It is a rare occurrence to have every member of House of Wells together. But we managed it one Fourth of July for a picnic in our backyard. I was sitting at a table with a few of the grandkids and noticed something.

I noticed something about Lucas.

I noticed something ON Lucas.

I squinted, leaned forward, stared for a few seconds, and asked, "Is that a... mustache?"

It was, indeed, a mustache. It was barely visible to the naked eye, but still it was there. Lucas grinned a satisfying grin. I think he wanted me to notice. Well, I did, and it was a good manly moment between Granddad and Grandson.

We are a collection of bearded men in the Wells Tribe and the Estep Clan, and Lucas is becoming one of them.

Time goes by so fast.

* * *

Children's children are a crown to the aged.

Proverbs 17:6

Words of Wisdom

My young grandson Caleb and I were waiting in the car while his mom and granny were shopping.

I thought it was a great time to impart some grandfatherly wisdom to him.

We joked about how long they were in the store, and we played a game where we counted people who went into the store after mom and granny and then came out before mom and granny.

There were many people who did that. I informed him that this was not unusual and he should get used to it.

And then Caleb said something that revealed his superior intelligence. He said, "Do you think it is just in their nature to take a long time to shop?"

Yes, grasshopper, it is.

* * *

Love is patient, love is kind.

I Corinthians 13:4

Paris Can Wait

I have a niece named Piper Grace. Isn't that a pretty name?

She is a pretty, little girl with a beautiful personality.

When she was a 7-year-old, she was learning to recite John 3:16. She, as most children do, had some difficultly with a word or two.

She got the first part right, but the second part was just a little different.

She said, "For God so loved the world that He gave His only begotten Son, that whoever believes in Him *shall not go to Paris*, but have everlasting life."

Well, Piper, I do not want to go to Paris, either. I want to go to. . . the New Jerusalem!

* * *

Since, then, you have been raised with Christ, set your hearts on things above, where Christ is seated at the right hand of God. Set your minds on things above, not on earthly things. For you died, and your life is now hidden with Christ in God.

Colossians 3:1-3

A Little Boy's Confession

Cynthia, a dear lady in the Church I serve, worked in the cafeteria of our elementary school for many years, and she has many good stories.

She told me the story of Miss Betty, who had to speak with a little boy about his behavior toward a little girl.

The boy said, "I never said I was going to hit her."

Another girl spoke up and said, "Yes he did Miss Betty."

To which the boy retorted, "How do you know? You weren't even there when I said it."

Thanks Cynthia.

Just a cute story to brighten your day.

* * *

And he took the children in his arms, put his hands on them and blessed them.

Mark 15:16

It Got Out of the Way!

During one of my Bible Story Sessions with the Little Theologians of EduCare Preschool, I reviewed some of the stories we had discussed during the previous several weeks.

We reviewed Adam and Eve, Noah and the Ark, David and Goliath and a few more, including Moses and the Red Sea.

When I asked, "Do you recall what happened when Moses and the Children of Israel were at the Red Sea?"

One little girl spoke right up. She said, "Yeah, it got out of the way."

The most gifted scholar could not have said it better.

I love the way kids see things and say things.

* * *

Then Moses stretched out his hand over the sea, and all that night the LORD drove the sea back with a strong east wind and turned it into dry land. The waters were divided, and the Israelites went through the sea on dry ground, with a wall of water on their right and on their left.

Exodus 14:21, 22

Knowing Your Strengths

When I was growing up in Romney, West Virginia, I played Little League Baseball every summer. I played shortstop for the White Sox, and I still have some vivid memories of good times at the ball field. I also remember one player for the Cardinals.

Steve was not a power hitter, but he was fast as lightning, and I hated to see him come up to bat. You see, Steve knew his strengths and his weaknesses; he knew what he could do, and he knew what he could not do. He almost always bunted, and he almost always got on base. If you played him for the bunt, he would then just slap the ball right by you.

We are all gifted in different ways. Some of us may hit home runs, and some of us are better suited to bunt. Our goal should be to do what we do for the glory of God.

* * *

There are different kinds of gifts, but the same Spirit. There are different kinds of service, but the same Lord. There are different kinds of working, but the same God works all of them in all men. Now to each one the manifestation of the Spirit is given for the common good.

I Corinthians 12:4-7

Look What God Paid for Us

I read about an auction that took place in 1996. It was expected to bring in five million dollars, but on the first night alone it took it over four million dollars.

Someone paid $33,350 for a footstool; another person paid $48,875 for a tape measure. A tobacco humidor? $574.500!

The footstool was just a piece of furniture and the tape measured inches, feet and yards just like one you can buy for a few bucks. There was nothing special about the humidor.

So why did people spend so much money on them? Because of the one to whom they belonged. They belonged to President John F. Kennedy.

Consider: We belong to God. Look what He paid for us.

* * *

For you know that it was not with perishable things such as silver or gold that you were redeemed from the empty way of life handed down to you from your forefathers, but with the precious blood of Christ, a lamb without blemish or defect.

I Peter 1:18, 19

Spending Time with Yourself

My good friend Mark is an avid hunter. One day while visiting him and his wife Mary, I noted that deer season was fasting approaching and asked him if was ready to go.

"Yeah! I need some time to be with me,"

Some people may not understand his answer, but I do. Some may be uncomfortable being *with* themselves *by* themselves.

The Bible speaks about the need for solitude and silence. Even Jesus often withdrew to lonely places and prayed.

Luke 5:16

* * *

In repentance and rest is your salvation, in quietness and trust is your strength.

Isaiah 30:15

* * *

The LORD is my shepherd, I shall not be in want. He makes me lie down in green pastures, he leads me beside quiet waters, he restores my soul.

Psalm 23:1-3

Being the Church To the Church

He stopped in to see me one morning. I met him at the front door of the Church Building. We went into my study. We both sat in rockers. My rockers have a lot of miles on them. Some serious stuff has been discussed in them.

He stopped by for two reasons. The second reason was the best reason.

He had some good news he wanted to tell me personally. And it was good news. *Very* good news. When he was ready to leave, I prayed with him, thanking God for the very good news.

As we walked into the foyer toward the doors, he said four words. Four words I never tire of hearing. He said, "I love this place."

And then he added, "I really do."

Church: God's people being God's people to God's people.

* * *

"Therefore, as we have opportunity, let us do good to all people, especially to those who belong to the family of believers."

Galatians 6:10

Rationalizing Sin

One of my favorite shows growing up was *Leave It to Beaver*. It still is.

In one episode, Beaver, Wally and Eddie Haskell are going to the movies to see *The Voodoo Curse*.

But Mrs. Cleaver tells them to see *Pinocchio*.

As they approach the ticket booth, Eddie suggests a way around the problem. He says to Wally, "Your mom told you not to take the Beaver to 'The Voodoo Curse,' but what if the Beaver takes you?"

And with that bad bit of logic they convince themselves they are doing nothing wrong and they see *The Voodoo Curse*.

I think we all have a little bit of Eddie living inside us.

* * *

Now the serpent was more crafty than any of the wild animals the LORD God had made.

He said to the woman, "Did God really say, 'You must not eat from any tree in the garden?

The woman said to the serpent, "We may eat fruit from the trees in the garden, but God did say, 'You must not eat fruit from the tree that is in the middle of the garden, and you must not touch it, or you will die.'"

"You will not surely die," the serpent said to the woman.

"For God knows that when you eat of it your eyes will be opened, and you will be like God, knowing good and evil."

Genesis 3:1-5

Get Out!

During the pandemic of 2019, my wife Karen had two tests done at two different hospitals on two different days.

When we arrived for the first test, we put on our masks and went to the first check point where they asked questions and took our temperatures. I asked the young man if I could go with her, and he said I could.

At the next check point, however, I was abrasively **told** to leave the hospital and wait in the car by a woman whose people skills were... lacking. So I left.

A few days later at the second hospital, we put on our masks and went inside, where a friendly young man very politely, and apologetically, **asked** me to wait in the car. I told him I understood and it was no problem.

I did not mind being asked to get out by that young man, but I did not like being told to get out by that lady It is usually not a matter of what you say, but how you say it.

***

A gentle answer turns away wrath, but a harsh word stirs up anger.

Proverbs 15:1

The Rock

I grew up on Second Street in Romney, West Virginia.

It was a great place to be a kid. We had woods, embankments, cliffs, and a stream running through the valley floor. We also had a rock; a special rock that jutted out at an angle from the cliff.

We called it the "Slanted Rock." From it we hurled rocks at enemy soldiers approaching below and kept watch for dangerous animals on the prowl. Slanted Rock was a safe place to be and the view was good.

The Bible reminds us that God is our Rock.

And the view is very good, indeed.

* * *

The LORD is my rock, my fortress and my deliverer; my God is my rock, in whom I take refuge.

Psalm 18:2

* * *

Truly he is my rock and my salvation; he is my fortress, I will never be shaken.

Psalm 62:2

On Being the Chosen Ones

I had to go to a certain place where you have to go through a security check. I had to empty your pockets, get wanded by a metal detector, etc. It was a good thing to do, considering the building.

While I was waiting my turn, I noticed that several people bypassed the security line and walked right into the building. They were important looking people, dressed in suits and carrying briefcases.

Now I thought that this was unfair, so I made a cute remark to one of the very nice guards. I said, "So, they are the chosen ones."

I was still permitted to enter the building.

I got to thinking about the "chosen ones."

Christians are called that. Peter writes, "But you are a chosen people, a royal priesthood, a holy nation, a people belonging to God, that you may declare the praises of him who called you out of darkness and into his wonderful light.

I Peter 2:9

You know, it IS good to be the "Chosen Ones."

No Other Name

No other name, no other name,
no other name can save us.
No other name, no other name,
no other name but Jesus.

No other name under heaven,
can bless with such wonderful peace.
No other name can calm the heart,
and cause our fears to cease.

No other name has such power,
to rescue us from hell.
No other name can take us
to heaven to eternally dwell.

No other name, no other name,
no other name can save us.
No other name, no other name,
no other name but Jesus.

* * *

She will give birth to a son, and you are to give him the name Jesus, because he will save his people from their sons.

Matthew 1:21

Salvation is found in no one else, for there is no other name under heaven given to men by which we must be saved.

Acts 4:12

Watching Two Games at Once

Have you ever tried to watch two ballgames at once?

It's not unusual.

I recall one particular time I watch two games at once. One game was a preseason contest between the Washington Redskins and the Baltimore Ravens which aired on ESPN.

The other game was a Little League World Series game pitting the Keystone Little League of Clinton County, Pennsylvania against Huntington Beach, California on ESPN2.

I nearly wore out the remote going back and forth, back and forth, back and forth.

Well, it turned out that I enjoyed neither game, and it was not because both of my teams lost.

It was because I failed to choose one.

Changing from one channel to another repeatedly left me unable to appreciate either game.

I never stayed on one game long enough to really get into it.

I simply saw the scores and parts of plays - a hit here, a pass there. I experienced none of the drama of the contests; could not participate in the narrative, as I had done in earlier LLWS games involving the boys from Keystone.

There is a life lesson and a Biblical truth in this story.

* * *

But if serving the LORD seems undesirable to you, then choose for yourselves this day whom you will serve, whether the gods your forefathers served beyond the River, or the gods of the Amorites, in whose land you are living. But as for me and my household, we will serve the LORD.

Joshua 24:15

* * *

No one can serve two masters. Either you will hate the one and love the other, or you will be devoted to the one and despise the other.

Matthew 6:24

Cheer for the Church!

Cheer for the Church, you people of God,
cheer for the Church without shame;
or Christ is pleased to save us from sin,
by the power of His magnificent Name.

Cheer for the Church, you people of God,
cheer for the Church with delight;
for Christ is preparing our homes above,
our future is good and bright

* * *

We live in a time when the Church is not appreciated like it once was. I suppose every generation of Christians can say that.

We have our faults and shortcomings, to be sure. It is an easy thing for critics to say, "The Church is full of hypocrites."

But I prefer to see the Church as described in the Bible.

Paul wrote, "Praise be to the God and Father of our Lord Jesus Christ, who has blessed us in the heavenly realms with every spiritual blessing in Christ. For he chose us in him before the creation of the world to be holy and blameless in his sight."

Ephesians 1:3, 4

***

Now you are the body of Christ, and each one of you is a part of it.

I Corinthians 12:27

***

Although I hope to come to you soon, I am writing you these instructions so that, if I am delayed, you will know how people ought to conduct themselves in God's household, which is the church of the living God, the pillar and foundation of the truth.

I Timothy 3:14, 15

Faith Always Trusts

We must take care that God is the object of our faith. Some seem to think *faith* is the *object* of our faith, and that God is obligated to grant every we wish for. Biblical faith is tested, tried, sometimes tortured. It refuses to give up, even when God seems silent.

> Faith does not always know
> what God is going to do,
> but faith always trusts
> that He is faithful and true.
>
> In this wicked world
> we fight faithfully to the end,
> and eagerly await the crown
> He gives us when we win.

* * *

Now faith is being sure of what we hope for and certain of what we do not see. This is what the ancients were commended for.

Hebrews 11:1, 2

* * *

Consider it pure joy, my brothers, whenever you face trials of many kinds, because you know that the testing of your faith develops perseverance.

James 1:2, 3

Just Say the Word, Lord.

One of the best expressions of faith in the Gospels comes from an unexpected soul.

In Matthew 8:8, Roman soldier approaches Jesus seeking healing for his servant. Jesus offers to go to his house, but the centurion replies, "Lord, I do not deserve to you have you come under my roof. But just say the word, and my servant will be healed."

And Jesus is "astonished," and brags about this man's faith.

When God speaks, things happen!

* * *

Just say the word, Lord, just say the word.
All things come to pass, Lord,
when Your voice is heard.
Nothing can withstand, Lord,
when Your blessings are conferred
So just say the word, Lord, just say the word.

* * *

When God speaks, things happen!

"By faith we understand that the universe was formed at God's command, so that what is seen was not made out of what was visible.

Hebrews 11:3

You Are Not Going to Believe This

I received a call from Karen. Her first words were, "You are not going to believe this."

Now I do not know about you, but I do not like a conversation to begin with those words. I have heard them many times:

- "You are not going to believe this, but the delivery truck just took out a portion of our fence."

- "You are not going to believe this, but they delivered a damaged stove...again."

- "You are not going to believe this, but the doctor sent my prescription to the wrong pharmacy. . . again."

So, I was braced for more bad news.

Then Karen said, "I was going through the back of a closest (I was braced for the worst) and I found two Christmas gifts for you -from 2016" (this was 2018).

One of my favorite words is *serendipity*, and that was good, serendipitous news. when I arrived home that evening, I had two Christmas gifts waiting for me.

I wonder, when we get to Heaven, will the Lord say, "You are not going to believe this, but. . .

I have *this* place prepared just for you."

* * *

And if I go and prepare a place for you, I will come back and take you to be with me that you also may be where I am.

John 14:3

* * *

"Surely goodness and love will follow me all the days of my life, and I will dwell in the house of the LORD forever.

Psalm 23:6

* * *

As a prisoner for the Lord, then, I urge you to live a life worthy of the calling you have received. Be completely humble and gentle; be patient, bearing with one another in love.

Ephesians 4:1,2

Holy Hypocrisy, Batman!

I pulled up to the stop light. In front of me was a car with a breast cancer awareness license plate. On the plate were the words: Educate. Advocate. Eradicate.

When the light turned green, we pulled out and I passed her. I looked over and saw something I did not expect: A woman puffing away on a cigarette. I thought, "There is definitely something wrng with this picture."

Now, for most of the day I "meditated" on that contradiction, how she did not present a good example, considering what was on her license plate.

And, at some point, this came to mind, "You hypocrite, first take the plank out of your own eye, and then you will see clearly to remove the speck from your brother's eye.

Matthew 7:5

***

Each one should test his own actions. Then he can take pride in himself, without comparing himself to somebody else, for each one should carry his own lead.

Galatians 6:5

Hatin' Life?

Over the years I have seen some pretty good vanity plates, as I am sure you have. Some encouraging. Some funny. Some with Bible verse. Some rather nasty. Vanity plates are designed to declare a message, to reveal something about the owner of the vehicle.

I saw this tag: H8NLIFE. I did a double take. The owner of that vehicle was broadcasting to everyone his feelings about life. I wondered what this person experienced in life? What is he going through? How has he been hurt?

But there is another possibility: A disciple of Jesus, who takes the Lord's words seriously:

The man who loves his life will lose it, while the man who hates his life in this world will keep it for eternal life.

John 12:25

Do not love the world or anything in the world. If anyone loves this world, the love of the Father is not in him. For everything in the world—the cravings of the sinful man, the lust of his eyes and the boasting of what he has and does—comes not from the Father but from the world. The world and its desires pass away, but the man who does the will of God lives forever."

I John 1:15-17

How Long Will She Be in Heaven

A young girl named Sarah was getting ready to be baptized. She was very excited to obey Jesus.

Sarah's mother tried to explain to Sarah's 4-year-old sister, Jill, what Sarah was going to do.

Jill thought for a few moments and asked, "How long will Sarah be gone to heaven to see Jesus?"

I have said it before and I will say it again: I love the way kids see things and say things.

One of these days, either by way of death or the Return of Christ, we will see Jesus face to face, and we will be with Him forever.

The question for us now is: Are we ready?

* * *

We live by faith, not by sight. We are confident, I say, and would prefer to be away from the body and at home with the Lord.

II Corinthians 5:7,8

The Right Car at the Right Time

One morning I was driving from Wise to Norton and I had something weighing on my mind when **Romans 8:28** came to mind, "And we know that in all things God works for the good of those who love him, who are called according to his purpose.

The Spirit of God loves to bless the Church of God with the Word of God.

I was approaching a stop light when a black SUV passed me. Now there are many black SUVs in the area but this one I had seen at least once before, and now, at this time and at this place, I saw it again.

With its license plate: 8 28 ROM.

Coincidence? I think not. God used the mobile ministry of that black SUV to gently reaffirm His presence and His promise.

It was as if God winked at me.

* * *

He guides the humble in what is right and teaches them his way. All the ways of the LORD are loving and faithful; for those who keep the demands of his covenant.

Psalm 25:9, 10

The Iceberg Metaphor

You have seen depictions of icebergs showing the top above water and the bottom in the water. Nearly ninety percent of it is below the water.

We only see the "tip of the iceberg."

This has become a metaphor for many things, including the practice of homiletics, the science and art of preaching, which I write about later in this book.

Most of sermon preparation is left in the study, and only a fraction is taken to the pulpit.

If a preacher delivered everything connected to a sermon it would be long, technical, overwhelming and extremely bor-ing!

The message you hear on Sunday mornings is only the tip of the iceberg.

A preacher has to know what to say and what NOT to say.

I was taught in basic homiletics that for every minute in the pulpit delivering the sermon the preacher should spend an hour in the study preparing the sermon.

In my forty-seven years of preaching, I have found this to be generally true.

The "Iceberg Metaphor" may not be a perfect metaphor, but true enough for many areas of life.

Most of our preparation and training for life takes place below the surface, behind the scenes, and on the inside, as we quietly and faithfully abide in Christ, and He in us.

* * *

Abide in me and I in you.

As the branch cannot bear fruit of itself, unless it abides in the vine, neither can you, unless you abide in Me.

I am the vine, you are the branches.

He who abides in Me, and I in him, bears much fruit; for without Me you can do nothing.

John 15:4, 5, NKJV

New King James Version ®
Copyright © 1982 by Thomas Nelson.
Used by permission. All rights reserved.

A Great Question to Think About

A local Church had this on their marquee: If you knew Jesus was coming tomorrow, what would you do today?"

Think about that question. What WOULD you do today if you knew, for certain, that the Lord was coming back tomorrow?

Jesus tells us that no one knows when it will happen, but the question is good to consider. So, if you knew Jesus was coming tomorrow, what would you do today?

I would weep with joy!

* * *

But concerning that day and hour no one knows, not even the angels of heaven, nor the Son, but the Father only.

Matthew 24:36

"So you must be ready, because the Son of Man will come at an hour when you do not expect him.

Matthew 24:44

Therefore keep watch, because you do not know the day or the hour.

Matthew 25:13

The Unholy Car

A while back I saw a car with a sticker I had never seen on a vehicle before. I was driving home and listening to Third Day's moving rendition of "Agnus Dei," and I pulled up behind a car with a sticker that read "unholy."

Just as Third Day was singing "You are Holy, Holy. I saw the "unholy" sticker.

The unholy car went straight to "wherever" and I turned right. I have not seen that car since. It had out of state tags, so perhaps it was just passing through on it's way to "wherever" it seems to be going.

Many things and many souls pass through this life with unholy intentions but not everyone so advertises. Unholy things can be clever and subtle, lying-in wait for an unsuspecting soul. The Bible tells to be alert and on guard, for our enemy the devil is on the prowl. There is a lot of unholiness out there.

And one more thing: God tells us to *be* holy.

* * *

But just as he who called you is holy, so be holy in all you do."

I Peter 1:15

"He Did That for Us?"

A few years ago, during the Resurrection Season, one of our Disciple School Teachers was talking with her little students about Jesus, and how He died on the cross for our sins.

She told them that God loves us so much that He gave up His only Son so we can go to heaven to be with Him.

One little girl began to cry.

With tears running down her little cheeks, she said, "He did that for us?"

Yes. Yes He did.

* * *

For God so loved the world that he gave his one and only Son, that whoever believes in him shall not perish but have eternal life.

John 3:16

* * *

This is how we know what love is: Jesus Christ laid down his life for us.

I John 3:16

The Perfect Name for a Cemetery

A few years ago, I was listening online to WMAL, a radio station out of Washington, DC. They air commercials, of course.

There was a commercial about the Catholic cemeteries of the Archdiocese of Washington.

They have interesting names:

- Mt. Olive Cemetery.
- All Souls Cemetery.
- St. Mary's Cemetery.
- Gate of Heaven Cemetery.

But the one I like the best has an excellent name for a cemetery: Resurrection Cemetery!

Isn't that a cool name for a cemetery!

***

For the Lord himself will come down from heaven, with a loud command, with the voice of the archangel and with the trumpet call of God, and the dead in Christ will rise first. After that, we who are still alive and are left will be caught up together with them in the clouds to meet the Lord in the air. And so we will be with the Lord forever. Therefore encourage each other with these words.

I Thessalonians 4:16-18

What a Way to Put It

During the Resurrection Season a few years ago I put my research team I call The Little Theologians of EduCare Preschool to work.

I was not able to be with them that day so I asked our Director to record their comments about Easter.

They were asked: What happened on Easter?

They said:

- He rode a camel on Friday.

- They put thorns on His head.

- They whipped Him.

- They poked Him on His side.

- He died on the cross.

- He loves us.

- He got in a cave.

- They put a big bolder in front of the tomb.

- The angel at the tomb said, "He is not here."

And one of the four-year-old boys described the resurrection this way: "Three days after, He raised up and got out!"

"He raised up and got out!" I love the way kids see things and say things.

This makes me wonder. What if?

What if God had sent angels in the form of children to announce the Good News to the women?

Instead of saying, "Why do you seek the living among the dead? He is not here; he has risen," perhaps they would have said, "He raised up and got out!"

* * *

For what I received I passed on to you as of first importance: that Christ died for our sins according to the Scriptures, that he was buried, that he was raised on the third day.

I Corinthians 15:3

* * *

And if Christ has not been raised, our preaching is useless and so is your faith.

I Corinthians 15:14

The Best Thanksgiving Answer

When Thanksgiving comes around, our EduCare Preschool Staff and I ask my little theologians what they want to thank God for and we received many honest and humorous answers over the years.

- "Soccer."
- "My house."
- "My dirt bike."
- "Running fast."
- "Gus" (her dog),
- "Girl football."
- "The McDonald's slide."
- "Dogs, cats, mom and dad" (notice the order).

The one that touched my heart the most came from a little girl who said, "For Jesus and that He hung there."

* * *

Let us fix our eyes on Jesus, the author and perfecter of our faith, who for the joy set before him endured the cross, scorning its shame, and sat down at the right hand of the throne of God."

Hebrews 12:2

Are You Thankful for You?

Several years ago, during our Thanksgiving Youth Night, when we broke into age groups for special activities and the kids made a cross on which they wrote blessing for which they were grateful.

And as is so often the case, a few of the kids forgot theirs and we would find them here and there in the building.

Later, I was in the Church office doing some copying and I found a cross which was left behind. And I was blessed and encouraged when I read, "I am thankful for me."

I thought how appropriate. This young person is thankful to God for her!

Are you thankful for you?

Are you thankful that God made you and called you into fellowship with Him, forgave you, saved you, blessed you?

* * *

In him we were also chosen, having been predestined according to the plan of him who works out everything in conformity with the purpose of his will.

Ephesians 1:11

When Jesus Showed Up

There is a story that takes place in heaven.

God and an angel are talking about a man who had lived an especially horrible life. God is about to welcome him into heaven.

The angel objects, insisting the man is not fit to enter. He points out the man's millions of sins and faults. God listens patiently. Seeing he is getting nowhere, he says to God, "O Lord, can't you see what kind of man he is?"

To which God replies, "No. I can't. Jesus is in the way."

* * *

All we like sheep had gone astray,
and the price for sin we could not pay.
But praise be to God for that incredible day
when Jesus showed up and got in the way.

* * *

The Word became flesh and made his dwelling among us. We have seen his glory, the glory of the One and Only, who came from the Father, full of grace and truth.

John 1:14

And It Came to Pass

And it came to pass once on the earth,
a gift of eternal worth,
given in Messiah's birth,
it came to pass once on the earth.

This Good News of Great Joy, t
he incarnation of the Baby Boy,
and Satan tried to destroy
this Good News of Great Joy.

Peace on earth, goodwill toward men,
was the reason for God to send,
the blessing that will never end, peace on
earth goodwill toward men.

Praise be to the Prince of Peace,
His government will increase,
His reign will never, ever cease,
praise be to the Prince of Peace.

Yes, it came to pass once on the earth.

* * *

But the angel said to them, "Do not be afraid. I bring you good news of great joy that will be for all the people. Today in the town of David a Savior has been born to you; he is Christ the Lord."

Luke 2:10, 11

A New Year's Prayer

For this New Year, Lord, we pray,
for your wisdom come what may.
We need your guidance for each day,
for this New Year, Lord, we pray.

For this New Year, Lord, we pray,
grant us grace in all we say.
Help us never from You to stray,
for this New Year, Lord, we pray.

* * *

Trust in the LORD with all your heart and lean not on your own understanding; in all your ways acknowledge him, and he will make your paths straight.

Proverbs 3:5,6

* * *

We live by faith, not by sight.

II Corinthians 5:7

Part Two
BIG Things

A BIG Thing is a short sermon summary, also called the Big Idea or the Main Idea, a variation of the more technical thesis statement or propositional statement which is taught in Homiletics 101.

Homiletics (from the Greek, homiletikos; a homily, a discourse, a sermon) is the branch of practical theology focusing on the science of sermon construction and the art of sermon delivery. It seeks to apply canonical rules of interpretation to a Biblical text, and principles of logical rhetoric to the practice of preaching

The following BIG Things are summary statements of two hundred of my sermons. You will notice that many BIG Things are of a common theme. That is because they are part of a particular "sermon series."

While based on specific Biblical texts and stories, these BIG Things are also "stand alone" truths and are useful for personal contemplation and spiritual formation.

They may also help preachers and teachers in their preparation of sermons and lessons.

1.
God's power and God's plan
come together when God's people pray.

2
Christian ministry to a corrupt culture takes
place by pointing people to faith in Christ
and providing people a place in Christ.

3
We minister TO a corrupt culture
by being a Sanctuary IN a corrupt culture.

4
I must do my duty as an alien in America
even though I'd rather be at home in Heaven.

5
The Church of Christ is the Body of Christ,
entrusted with the Gospel of Christ
until the return of Christ.

6.
Since the Church means so much to God,
I choose to make the Church mean more to me.

7
We glorify the Head of the Church
when we edify the members of the Church.

8
I choose to pray for my Church,
fellowship with my Church,
and minister to my Church.

9
I choose Church for the glory of my Lord,
the growth of my Faith,
and the good of my Family.

10
The Church is
the best group of people *in* the world
with the greatest message *to* the world
with the best future *out of* this world.

11
We minister to souls one soul at a time.

12
The Church provides a positive place
in a negative world.

13
The Church builds people up
in a world that tears people down.

14
God's grace puts us in our place,
and God's grace keeps us in our place.

15
All Christians are set apart
by the Spirit of God
to perpetually glorify the Son of God.

16
Many are invited but few are chosen
to receive so great a salvation,
because only a few choose to be chosen
by accepting God's invitation.

17
Let us use both words and deeds
to keep on sowing Kingdom Seeds.
In prayer and patience give our best,
and let Him worry about the rest.

18
Christians are not responsible
for growing seeds, but we are
responsible for sowing seeds.

19
We reach out to help others reach up.

20
A healthy Church knows two facts
that she must faithfully uphold:
Satan is on the prowl,
but God is in control.

21
Spiritually healthy Churches are made up
of spiritually healthy Christians.

22
A Church's spiritual health is directly related
to loving Christ first of all and best of all.

23
The hope of heaven is stronger
than the troubles we face on earth,
and the glory we will experience
is of everlasting worth.

24
The Church of Christ is
supposed to be different
and jealously guard when we preach;
we must never compromise our doctrines,
but zealously guard what we teach.

25
Tolerance of sin leads to sin
and arrogantly betrays the Lord,
Who calls His Church to be holy and distinct,
and obedient to His Word.

26
Sometimes a good reputation is dead wrong
and repentance is what God requires;
and the only thing that should matter to us
is what the Head of the Church desires.

27
Small spiritually growing Churches
can do BIG things,
because small, spiritually growing
Churches serve a BIG God.

28
The Church is to BE
the Church TO the Church.

29
Joy is the calm, confident attitude of good
cheer, knowing that in God's time and in
God's way, everything is going to be OK.

30
We are experts in sin,
but God is an expert in grace.

31
Baptism is a reasonable response
to the grace of God.

32
Communion is a time to remember,
reflect, repent, receive and rejoice.

33
We must first say "yes" to the Spirit
in order to say "no" to the flesh.

34
If I want to trust the Lord with all my heart,
I need to give the Lord all my heart,
so He can clean up all my heart.

35
As God's workmanship in Christ,
we've been created in Christ,
to be conformed to the likeness of Christ,
all for the glory of Christ.

36
God spiritually forms us in Christ
when we make every effort
to live a live worthy of our calling in Christ.

37
Spiritual formation of the Body happens
when each member of the Body
does its work according to the gifts
of grace each member has.

38
The Lord uses all situations,
relationships and callings
for the spiritual formation
of the Members of His Church.

39
For spiritual formation to happen, God's
armor we daily must wear;
each piece has a specific purpose
and must faithfully be used in prayer.

40
I do not have to understand
God's mysterious ways
in order to give Him glory and praise.

41
Only by the light of God's Word
can we see the devil's lies.

42
The longer I live in this world,
the more I do not belong.
I am a stranger in this foreign land,
and being here seems wrong.
I have never seen my home,
but cannot wait to get there,
to add my voice to countless souls
God's praises to declare.

43
Good faith submits an unknown future
to an all-knowing God.

44
Faith is needed the most
when we wait on God the most.

45
Jesus will come in great glory and power,
but no one will know the day or the hour.

46
When Judgment Day comes no one
will can accuse God of being unfair.

47
Hell is the logical place
for the logical punishment of all things evil.

48
No one in hell will say to God,
"I do not deserve this,"
and no one in heaven will say to God,
"I do deserve this."

49
Heaven is an imagination defying place,
prepared for God's people
who are saved by God's grace.

50
If Jesus forgives these sins of mine,
I can forgive anyone, of anything, anytime.

51
God uses bad times to grow good faith.

52
A thousand lies told by Satan
cannot undo one truth told by God.

53
If you want to get the most out of your life,
make sure Christ is Lord of your life.

54
We are who we are because He is who He is.

55
If I want Monday through Saturday
to be better days, I must choose to make
Sunday the best day.

56
Knowing where we are going
helps us to live where we are living.

57
My life may be complicated and tough,
but God's grace is more than enough.

58
All we like sheep had gone astray
and the cost for sin we could not pay,
but praise be to God or that incredible day
when Jesus showed up and got in the way.

59
I do not know what tomorrow holds,
whether I will live or die;
but I do not the One who knows all things,
the what, the when and the why.

60
God's love is unconditional,
God's salvation is not.

61
My understanding is very limited,
my knowledge is so small;
but God knows what He is doing,
and by faith upon Him I call.

62
God places before us two ways to live
and tells us that we must decide;
I can trust in the ways of this foolish world,
or trust God to be by my side.

63
Sinful choices will lead to a life
of sad and terrible consequences;
but no one celebrates more than God
when a sinner comes to his senses.

64
In all things God works,
in all things God plans,
for all things we face,
are all in God's hands.

65
God knows who His people are,
in the midst of His Judgment Days;
and rejoices over His Faithful Few,
as we offer up our praise.

66
Our personal involvement
in the Mission is determined
by our personal belief in the Message.

67
Since each day could be my last,
I must prepare my soul to pass
from living in this sinful place,
to eternal glory, peace and grace.

68
In this world my life I hate,
for I do not belong;
my eyes are fixed on Heaven's Gate,
and my eternal Home.

60
A fool is a person
who stupidly orders his life
without regard to God's Wisdom
revealed in God's Word.

70
As we watch the Parade of Fools go by,
let's be wise and not join in;
for God tells us in His Word,
the cost of choosing sin.

71
A faith well believed is a faith well lived.

72
Fools build their lives on satanic lies,
and will eventually pay the price;
wise people build on God's truth,
which produces a fruitful life.

73
For my mind to have the peace of God,
it must be fixed on the God of peace.

74
We must live a life of repentance
and humbly seek His face;
and pray for ourselves and others,
for God to show mercy and grace.

75
My jar of clay will chip and crack,
but that will change with Christ comes back.

76
Lord is who He is;
Savior is what He does.

77
When a man walks out of His own grave,
we better listen to what He has to say.

78
We know that God knows,
and that is all we need to know.

79
God roughens our faith
to toughen our faith
so we will receive the goal of our faith.

80
God will bring us to a suffering place
so we can become strong
in His sufficient grace.

81
A holy life is a life
that thinks as Jesus thinks
and does what Jesus does.

82
My Heavenly Home is a place
that defies imagination;
and I will take my undeserved place
in God's eternal congregation.

83
When we wonder how much longer,
when we long for that Glorious Day;
remember we are not home yet,
but we are definitely on the way.

84
When the time comes for
Jesus to come back,
when He returns with His Heavenly Host;
no matter if I'm already in heaven
it is the thing that I want the most.

85
We are called to Keep Sunday Sacred
by eagerly and faithfully gathering
as the Lord's Family, on the Lord's Day,
at the Lord's Table, for the Lord's Glory.

86
The Church is spiritually one at all times,
and physically one at appointed times;
and to abandon the Church physically
endangers the Church spiritually.

87
We come to the Table every Lord's Day,
to glorify the Life, the Truth, and the Way.
We gather as Sheep, to heed His voice,
to proclaim His death, to repent and rejoice.

88
Gut check faith is simple, but strong;
I will not give up when life goes wrong.

89
Faith believes God is always good
even when things are temporarily bad.

90
We are to speak good things about God
even while experiencing bad things from God.

91
Faith believes life makes sense to God
even when it does not make sense to us.

92
When I leave my fragile tent on earth
and see my Lord upon His Throne;
I will cry out with my own people
"There is no place like home!"

93
Awaiting us as a gift of grace
are better times and a better place;
we are fed up with this earthly experience
but will overcome with patient persistence.

94
To be right with God
will cause you to be wrong with the world.

95
God's way may seem the long way,
but it is never the wrong way.

96
Enduring temptation results
in spiritual formation.

97
Jesus is not one of many,
He is the One and Only.

98
The big answer to the big question
determines where we will spend eternity.

99
No problem too big, so detail too small,
the God of the Bible is the God of them all.

100
When set apart by God,
do not behave like the devil.

101
God has a way of getting in the way
to do things His way.

102
Salvation is the blessed state
of being rescued by Jesus
FROM God's wrath and FOR God's work.

103
Whoever or whatever rules my heart
will determine my daily choices;
if God rules my heart then I'll
reject all other voices.

104
The world is worse than we think,
but heaven is better than we imagine.

105
Upon the cross God put to shame
the wisdom of humanity;
and firmly established for all time
the great doctrine of Christianity.

106
Doctrine really does matter, for what we
believe determines how we live.

107
When faced with options in our lives
that call upon us to choose;
choosing what gets us closer to Christ
is the wisest thing to do.

108
God sets before us two clear paths,
as different as day and night;
we can choose the path to spiritual darkness,
or the path to spiritual light.

109
The Doctrine of Jesus matters eternally
because it determines
where we will spend eternity.

110
When bad days come as they so often do,
three good words I must recall:
Providence, patience and perseverance,
will bless things great and small.

111
Blessings: Just because we can't always see
them does not mean they are not there.

112
Grace enables us to suffer temporarily
FOR His glory so we will reign eternally
IN His glory.

113
We make a great mistake when we think
God thinks like we think.

114
Instead of being discouraged
by the uncommitted crowd,
I choose to be encouraged
by the committed core.

115
By virtue of His sacrificial death,
Jesus paid for our sins
and appeases God's wrath;
since He speaks to the Father
in our defense, we can approach
God's Throne in confidence.

116
Just say the word, Lord, just way the word;
all things come to pass, Lord,
when Your voice is heard.
Nothing can withstand, Lord,
when Your blessings are conferred;
so just say the word,
Lord, just say the word.

117
Faith does not always know
what God is going to do,
but faith always trusts
that He is faithful and true.

118
In this wicked world
we fight faithfully to the end,
and eagerly await the crown
He gives us when we win.

119
There are details in God's agenda
that may never come to light,
but He works them all together
so things will come out right.

120
Life is a series of temporary setbacks
leading to eternal victory.

121
My true identity is being a soul
saved by the Son of God,
connected to the Church of God,
equipped by the Spirit of God
to live for the glory of God.

122
We live faithfully IN this world
until God takes us OUT of this world.

123
No fear faith is a better way to live
than to faith fear.

124
Prayers of pain and prayers of praise
can come from the say heart at the same time.

125
When life happens from day to day,
and causes stress to come my way;
from my Lord I will not stray,
for in His will I want to stay.

126
God does not think like we think,
and great and mysterious are His ways;
faith does not demand all the answers,
even during the most difficult of days.

127
How we respond to the way of the wicked
is more important than understanding
the way of the wicked.

128
The way of the wicked is the devil's way,
it deceives and destroys the soul.
The way of the righteous is God's way,
and through Christ it makes us whole.

129
The wicked have no fear
of God to restrain them in their way;
and they will be judged accordingly
on the coming Judgment Day.

130
God's holiness demands the wicked
be judged in ways that may seem severe;
but we trust His perfect
knowledge and wisdom,
and by faith we can live without fear.

131
Focusing our faith in worship and praise
will put things in the proper light;
the way of the wicked will come to and end,
when God makes everything right.

132
The way of the wicked seems easy
and free from all despair,
but I choose to live by faith
and trust His providential care.

133
Because we are easily distracted
by lesser things,
God needs to remind us
of the best of things.

134
The Church is to do the right things even
when we do not see right results.

135
When we wait on God; we wait with God.

136
For me to do God's Will,
I must focus on God's Word.

137
Since each day could be my last day
I will not to this world cleave;
I must prepare my soul to pass;
I must always be ready to leave.

138
I will live a foolish life,
if I focus on foolish ways;
and be unable to stand before God
when I account for all my days.

139
Jesus saved me while I was dead in my sins,
so I will not be defined by my past;
in faith I press on one day at a time, for the
prize that forever will last.

140
Membership in a local church matters
Base local churches make up
THE Universal Church.

141
For me to live well in a world going to hell,
I must trust God and never depart;
and fix my mind on Him all the time,
and His peace will stand guard in my heart.

142
Knowing my place in this world
comes from knowing my place in Christ.

143
By standing strong IN the Lord,
we can stand strong FOR the Lord.

144
Knowing where we are going
helps us to live where we are living.

145
We must grow in the faith
and fight for the faith
so we do not fall from the faith.

146
Princes and peasants and all in between
will one day confess Jesus is King.

147
I choose to focus on Jesus Christ
and enjoy His affections,
so I will not be dragged around
in all different directions.

148
I am a citizen of heaven and
I cannot wait to get there;
but as an exile in a pagan land,
I will live in persistent prayer.

149
Being a member of the Lord's Church
is the biggest blessing and
highest honor I can receive...
and membership matters!

150
Membership in the Lord's Church
is to be taken as seriously
as the Lord takes it.

151
Membership in a Local Church matters
because local Churches make up
the universal Church.

152
Blaming unbelievers for declining
Church attendance is like blaming
strangers for not attending
your family reunions.

153
Hebrews 10:25 is written
to members of local Churches
who *have not* abandoned the Church
so they *will not* abandon the Church.

154
How faithful we are as members of the Church
is determined by how grateful
we are to the Lord of the Church.

155
Local Churches, despised by the world,
are God's chosen vessels
for reaching the world,
and every member
is a minister in the mission.

156
My membership in the Church matters
because of WHO God says I am and WHAT
God says I do.

157
The local Church is God's divine design
and my membership must matter.

158
Jesus Christ dying for my sins
is the all-compelling reason
for me to be an eager and faithful
member of His Church.

159
If you are not missed in Church,
perhaps you are not there
often enough to be missed.

160
Members of the Church are -

saved by the Son of God: new birth,
filled by the Spirit of God: new life,
part of the Family of God: new relationships,
instructed by the Word of God: new priorities,
to live for the glory of God: new purpose.

161
When God is with His people,
the improbable becomes probable,
and the impossible becomes possible.

162
Faith obediently trusts
God's Word will bring about
God's Will
for God's people
for God's glory.

163
Peace is the calm and confident attitude
of heavenly serenity which shepherds us to
our heavenly eternity.

164
The presence of God is real,
the power of God is absolute,
the providence of God is discernable and
the purpose of God is eternal.

165
The presence of the Lord, and the power of
the Lord, and the providence of the Lord, and
the purpose of the Lord all work together to
produce the JOY of the Lord.

166
We must daily ponder the presence,
power, providence and purpose of God
to daily experience the hope,
faith, peace and joy of God.

167
A confessing Church says what the state will
not say: Jesus Christ is the only way.

168
Holiness matters to God and
it must matter to me,
so I will live in such a way
for the wicked world to see.

169
As we serve the Lord in our place,
let us do so in love and grace.
May we model for others what it means
to serve and wait in "the in between."

170
Because of the birth in Bethlehem,
we have the hope of heaven.

171
God plans His work and works His plan
which one day we will see,
when Jesus returns to be glorified
for all eternity.

172
There are details about the Day of the Lord
that we simply cannot know,
but one thing that is plainly taught,
we must be ready to go.

173
A disciple is a born-again soul,
who lives a born-again life,
in order to be conformed
to the likeness of Christ.

174
A disciple is a saved, born-again soul,
who lives a saved born-again life,
whose relationships are prioritized
by his relationship with Christ.

175
To ask the Lord to bless a soul
is a serious thing to pray;
not something we vainly repeat
when we don't know what to say.

176
When I ask the Lord to lead, guide and direct,
He may lead me to a place I do not expect.
But wherever He leads, wherever He guides,
He will direct me through the grace He provides.

177
To keep us secure in Jesus
God warns us to be on guard,
for those who seek to ruin us,
and lure us away from the Lord.

178
My understanding is very limited,
my knowledge is so small;
but God knows what he is doing,
and by faith upon Him I call.

179
You can reach out without messing up by praying evangelistically, speaking clearly, and behaving wisely.

180
Let us *reach up* in eager worship,
reach in in faithful fellowship,
and *reach out* in loving service.

181
Let us simplify life, exemplify faith
and glorify God.

182
A heart that hungers for God is
heart that will worship God.

183
No matter how your life began,
no matter how unfair;
trust that God has a plan for you,
and seek that plan in prayer.

184
The right attitude comes from
following the right Person.

185
God can use bad situations for good reasons,
and bad people for good purposes.

186
Singing has nothing to do
with the quality of my voice,
but everything to do with
the worship of my heart.

187
If the heart is not right,
the worship is not right.

188
We must be more concerned
with what Jesus says about worship
than what we say about worship

189
Knowing where we are going
helps us to live where we are living.

190
There are details in God's agenda
that may never come to light,
but He works them all together
so things will come out right.

191
We walk by faith and not by sight,
in the brightest day and the darkest night.
No matter what life may hold,
it is comforting to know God's in control.

192
Jesus is the only answer bigger than any question,
the only solution bigger than any problem, and
the only Savior bigger than any sin.

193
Simply because people
do not love the God of love,
doesn't mean they *have not heard*
of the God of love.

194
To a world of lost souls let us be the Lord's
Church, calling sinners to repent of their sins.
But let's not neglect to be the Church TO the
Church, for at home is where love begins.

195
The wicked have no fear of God to
restrain their evil way,
and they will be judged accordingly
on the coming Judgment Day.

196
God's people must grow in the Faith
and fight for the Faith so we will
not fall from the Faith.

197
I cannot fight for the faith
if I am not equipped for the fight.

198
Jesus saved me while I was dead in my sins,
and I will not be defined by my past.
In focused faith I press on one day at a time,
for the prize that forever will last.

199
When we realize all the blessing
we have in Christ,
why wouldn't we want to grow in Christ?

200
For me to do God's Will
I must focus on God's Word.

Part III

Good Stuff for Your Soul

A collection of prose and poetry for personal pondering

Writing is good for the soul. At least I know it is good for my soul.

All of the joys and sorrows, victories and defeats, success and frustration of daily life spill out onto the page for me to revisit and reflect upon.

The act of writing, for me, is a form of contemplation, and in many ways prayer.

I have collected some of the anecdotes, remembrances, reflections and poems I have written over the years to share.

They chronicle my thoughts on a life of faith and family.

It is my prayer that you are as blessed by reading and thinking about these stories and poems as much as I was blessed to write them.

Ministry Moments

A few years ago I received a double blessing.

While in the Fellowship Hall the EduCare phone rang. It rings a lot during the summer months as parents prepare to enroll their children in the fall semester so I answered, "EduCare Preschool."

There was a woman on the other end inquiring about EduCare, saying that she has heard so many good things about our Preschool. I listened (with a smile on my face) and thanked her for her kind comments and I asked how she heard about our Preschool.

She told me through her friends. That was a blessing.

But she was not finished.

Recognizing my voice, she said how much she has enjoyed our "Bright Spots" radio ministry over the years, saying that they really are "Bright Spots." I smiled some more.

That was another blessing.

In the movie "Patton," the Allies were sweeping across Europe. General Patton was on the move. General Omar Bradley said,

"Give George a headline and he is good for another 30 miles."

It is good to receive blessings. They can come in many ways and from different people.

It is also good to give them. Let us be open to ministry moments when we can be a blessing to others.

Be Like Bill

Bill, 76 years old, loved to serve Communion at the Lord's Table at Norton Christian Church during our 8:45 Worship Service. He had a deep, husky voice and his prayers were very moving.

Bill developed some health problems which made it difficult for him to walk.

One Sunday morning I said, "Bill, I think we will give you a break from serving for a while, until you get stronger."

He replied, "Whatever you think best, preacher."

So a few months went by and Bill told me that he believed he was strong enough to serve.

I replied, "I don't know about that Bill. I think

I would feel better if you had a note from your doctor.

Next Sunday Bill had a note from his doctor.

It was one of the coolest things I have ever seen. That is how badly Bill wanted to serve the Lord's Supper to the Lord's People.

Not long after that, Bill was called Home.

Do You Have a Song

I received a call from a good friend who wanted to know if there was a particular song that has spoken to me over the years; a song that provides strength and comfort.

I told him there are three hymns that have been good TO me and good FOR me over the years:

- Joyful, Joyful, We Adore Thee
- O, For a Thousand Tongues to Sing
- A Mighty Fortress is Our God.

I said if I had to choose I would choose *A Mighty Fortress is Our God.*

He asked why and I said it is a majestic song containing great theology and it was written by an incredible man during desperate times.

A MIGHTY FORTRESS IS OUR GOD
Written by Martin Luther

A Mighty Fortress is our God,
a Bulwark never failing;
our Helper He amid the flood,
of mortal ills prevailing.

For still our ancient foe
doth seek to work us woe;
his craft and power are great,
and armed with cruel hate,
on earth is not his equal.
Did we in our own strength confide,
our striving would be losing;
were not the right Man on our side,
the Man of God's own choosing.
Dost ask who that may be?
Christ Jesus it is He;
the Lord of Hosts His Name,
from age to age the same,
and He must win the battle.

And though this world with devils filled,
should threaten to undo us.
We will not fear for God hath willed His truth
to triumph through us.
The prince of darkness grim,
we tremble not for him:
his rage we can endure,
for lo, His doom is sure;
one little word shall fell him.

That word above all earthly powers,
no thanks to them, abideth;
the Spirit and the gifts are ours
through Him who with us sideth.
Let goods and kindred go,
this mortal life also;
the body they may kill,
God's truth abideth still:
His Kingdom is forever.

A Snake in the Grass

It is well known among our Church Family that I am a snake-ophobe. The technical term is Ophidiophobe, but I prefer my own word, for it leaves no doubt what I am talking about and it is easier to pronounce.

My philosophy is also well known among my family and friends: "The only good snake is a dead snake."

One of my favorite riddles is: "What is better than a dead snake? Two dead snakes."

One night about 10:30 I took Gracie the Dog out to the backyard to do what Gracie the Dog does at 10:30 in the evening.

Anyway, about twenty feet away in the dimly lit grass I saw a snake; a thick snake, if stretched straight, would be at least 3 – 4 feet long.

Even Gracie acted a little skittish. After she finished I took her back inside and went to the other side of the house to get my trusty snake-killer (a flat head shovel) to apply my preferred form of snake execution; beheading, followed by a thorough dismemberment of the rest of the creature. With shovel in hand I walked around to engage the serpent.

As I slowly approached it I noticed that….it was a long clump of grass! I had mowed a few days before when the grass was wet.

I thought I saw a snake and I reacted accordingly.

I was, however, deceived.

The distance from the object and the lack of light on the subject tricked me into misinterpreting what I saw. Once I got closer and the light was better, I saw it for what it really was. He who has ears to hear, let him hear.

Time and again the Bible warns us, "Do not be deceived!"

One more thing: At least it was a clump grass I thought was a snake and not a snake I thought was a clump of grass!

This Is the Day the LORD Has Made

It was January 11, 2011. I was driving to the Church Building one morning and it was a cold, cloudy morning with snow on the ground with more on the way. About a half mile from my house I stopped was stopped at a traffic light. I sighed and quoted out loud Psalm 118:24: "This is the day the LORD has made, let us rejoice and be glad in it."

But I did not speak those words with a lot of enthusiasm, if you know what I mean. In fact, I was rather sarcastic. I did not FEEL like rejoicing.

Then I turned on the radio to our local K-Love station and they were talking about the numerical significance of today: 1-11-11. They mentioned how some people find that fascinating and others see nothing noteworthy about it. I suppose it is kind of interesting, but beyond that, no big deal. After all, yesterday was 1-10-11 and tomorrow will be 1-12-11. Does a digit really make one day any different than another?

But some good did come from my mental debate with the radio. I was reminded (by our patient Father) that each and every day is special and unique. Today will never be repeated, not because it is 1-11-11, but because it is today, a new day, different than yesterday and different than tomorrow. And because it is one of a kind it will fade into the past and another unique day will appear (if God wills) just as it has been doing since "in the beginning."

But one of these days You know Who will do you know what, and things will be changed forever. But until that day comes, we live by faith, one day at a time, each day, every day.

Yes, each day is holy, set apart by God. When we have an unhealthy focus on yesterday and tomorrow, we miss the here and now.

Perhaps that is what the Psalmist had in mind when he prayed, "THIS is the day!"

Not yesterday, not tomorrow, but "THIS is the day!" Live in today. Pray in today. Serve in today. Love in today. Wait in today.

This is the day God is God.

This is the day He cares for the birds of the air and clothes the grass of the field.

This is the day He "causes all things to work together for the good of those who love him."

This is the day He says, "I am with you always, to the very end of the age."

This is the day He says, "do not worry about tomorrow."

This is the day He says, "Behold, I am coming soon," and we say, "Amen. Come, Lord Jesus."

Psalm 90 is a prayer of Moses, who knew much about the passing of days. He said, "So teach us to number our days, that we may gain a heart of wisdom. How do we do that? How do we number our days? One day at a time.

When my mind is guided by faith rather than emotion, I can sing with David, without the sarcasm, "This IS the day the LORD has made. I will rejoice and be glad in it."

And I can sing, "Come, Lord Jesus!"

Serendipitous Small Things

It is a good thing to look for serendipitous moments in life. In as much that given the basic meaning of "serendipity," you can actually look for a serendipitous moment.

Anyway, I have had many such moments.

I was sitting in Studio C of WNVA doing my show "Grace Notes" when I looked out the window and saw it. It was a Rockwellian scene straight from an old December magazine cover.

The field behind the Studios and the woods surrounding Gay Dawn Acres were covered with a beautiful blanket of snow, and it was still coming down.

I was playing "Third Day's" Christmas CD when I decided to make a change in the lineup. I ran out to my car and grabbed a CD that Karen and I keep in the car during every Christmas Season and ran back into the Studio.

After the song that was playing finished, I flipped on the mic and announced, "I could not resist." and then I pushed play.

I sat back, looked out the window and listened (hopefully with many others) to "White Christmas" sung by Bing Crosby. It was a good three minutes.

Life is made up of big events, but also small moments. Perhaps the cumulative effect of small moments provides spiritual and emotional nourishment that help us face the big events.

The little things in life may more important than we think and bigger than we realize.

I recall a scene from "A Christmas Carol" when Ebenezer Scrooge, speaking to the Ghost of Christmas Past, said that the joy and fun Old Fezziwig provided were the result of "small things."

The Beast

I had one of my best serendipitous moments when I received word that it was time for our copier "from you know where" to be replaced.

It was my understanding that we would have to linger in purgatory two more years before this test of patience would end. But, no, I was wrong!

Five years went by faster than I realized.

When I received that call I almost wept. Yes, yes, yes, that demon possessed duplicator would soon be cast out of the church office.

Soon, the Beast, with the number "666" scribbled on it, would no longer tease and torture people who enter its horrible presence to beg for a copy like Oliver Twist asking for more gruel.

Soon, innocent souls would no longer have to tremble in its presence like Dorothy and her friends before the Wizard of Oz. Soon the smell of sulfur would be gone.

So, the Day of Jubilee arrived and we were delivered, and a new and improved machine began its duties at Norton Christian Church and I celebrated and went forth in joy, and thanked God for small mercies.

And there was peace among us.

Walla Walla!

Serendipitous moments can be welcomed detours in the day.

One happened a while back. It brought to mind something silly from 45 years ago. Remember that word silly, and all its synonyms (stupid, childish, inane, asinine, foolish, idiotic and juvenile) as you read this story.

Here is how it began. During the college football bowl season a few years ago a cute commercial aired. You probably remember it.

A police officer writes a speeding ticket. He hands it to the driver and says, "Roll Tide." The driver replies, "Roll Tide."

A mom drops her girls off at school. As they exit the minivan they say, "Roll Tide" and mom replies, "Roll Tide, y'all."

And a pastor ends a graveside benediction with "roll Tide, to which the mourners respond in unison, "Roll Tide."

I thought it was quite a clever tribute to the Crimson Tide of Alabama, and though I am a Mountaineer fan, I liked it and have jokingly said "Roll Tide" a few times.

But when I was a student at Eastern Christian College near Baltimore, a few friends and I had a word that we used at appropriate moments. It was our "Roll Tide."

"What was it?" you anxiously ask. Here it is, I hesitantly answer: "Walla!"

We may not have been the brightest of students.

I have no idea who among our inner circle at that small college started saying that word, and why that particular word was chosen. I give credit to either Mark or David. Or maybe both.

Anyway, it caught on and even one our professors humorously commented on it from time to time.

We used it as:

- A greeting: "Walla" we said as we passed in the halls.
- A term of uncertainty: Was lunch any good?" "Walla."
- An expression of frustration: "How did you do on the Greek test?" "Wallaaaaaa!"
- And as an affirmation: "Did you see the new girl on campus?" WALLA!
- And, of course, the first time I saw Karen, "WALLA! WALLA!!"

Now, was it dumb? Duh!

Immature? Of course.

Fun? Yes. It was fun.

What corny things are hiding in your youth that still make you smile?

Something to "walla" about...

Grace

Grace awake, grace asleep,
grace when troubles pile up deep.
Grace in good times, grace in bad,
grace when happy, grace when sad.

Grace in daylight, grace at night,
grace to carry on the fight.
Grace for husband, grace for wife,
grace for children all through life.

Grace when healthy, grace when hurt,
grace when rich or poor as dirt.
Grace for mind, and body and soul,
grace to heal and make me whole.

Grace to soothe my breaking heart,
grace to keep from falling apart.
Grace for present, grace for past,
grace to keep me to the last.

Grace to hold me in God's love,
grace to take me home above.
Grace in big things, grace in small,
grace from God, my all in all.

I Can't Wait

I can't wait to get there,
and meet the Lamb of God,
Who rescued me from my sins
and shed His sinless blood;
Whose lifeless body was entombed
that dark and terrible day,
waiting for that glorious morning
when death He cast away.

I can't wait to get there,
and see Him face to face,
to praise Him for His mercy,
to thank Him for His grace;
to fall before Him at His feet
and weep my tears of joy,
to bask in His eternal presence
which forever I'll enjoy.

I can't wait to get there,
I can't wait to see,
all the glorious blessings
He has prepared for me.
I can't wait to get there,
I can't wait to hear,
His kind and reassuring words,
"There is no need to fear."

I can't wait to get there,
I can't wait to know,
that all I learned and believed
is absolutely so;
to no longer live and walk by faith,
but forever more by sight,
where perfection will forever be,
and all is good and right.

So by my death or His Return,
I cannot wait to get there
and be in His eternal presence
and under His eternal care.

In the Silence of the Sanctuary

In the silence of the Sanctuary,
my soul retreats to pray;
I hear that holy hush,
I choose no words to say.
The sacred silence cleanses me o
f foolish, trivial nonsense,
and washes from my inner being
the residue of pretense.

In the silence of the Sanctuary,
my heart longs for peace;
my mind looks for rest,
and my worries seek release.
The thousand thoughts of my inner man
begin to shrink away,
as do the noise and clatter
of the crowded, busy day.

In the silence of the Sanctuary,
unspoken words I hear;
the warnings of the Prophets,
the Psalmist's joys and tears;
the longings of the faithful,
crying what and when and why?
I hear the Good News of the Gospels,
"Take courage, it is I."

In the silence of the Sanctuary,
I hear the ancient voices;
and join their sacred hymns,
in which my soul rejoices.
I hear the communion of the saints,
the echoes of their praise.
I hear the whispers of their hearts f
rom past and present days.

In the silence of the Sanctuary,
with my Lord I sit alone.
I still myself before Him,
He makes His presence known.
As I linger long with Him,
He casts away all fear,
And I grow in understanding
"Silence spoken here."

We Are Who We Are

We were eternally doomed,
we had hardness of heart;
we were helpless and hopeless
and utterly lost,
but His blood has set us apart.

We are the people of God,
we are forgiven of sin;
we are waiting to hear Him speak
the good words,
"Well done and come on in."

We are the saved and the sealed;
we are the salt and the light;
we trust and obey
and pray for the day
when our faith will give way to sight.

We are the Body of Christ,
we love the first day of the week;
we eagerly gather to honor His Name,
His will and wisdom to seek.

We are who we are,
because He is who He is,
and we're graced and blessed beyond belief
and the glory is eternally His.

Walk with Me

"Walk with Me," Jesus says,
"down that winding road.
Take my yoke upon you, child,
and I will share the load.

I will help you bear the burden;
I will help you all the way.
I will walk beside you,
each and every day."

"Walk with Me," Jesus says,
"walk with Me by faith.
You can trust what I teach,
my friend, you can trust what I say.

I am preparing a place for you, a
place of eternal worth,
a place beyond imagination,
a new heaven and a new earth."

"Walk with me," Jesus says,
"I will not let you down.
There will be difficult times ahead,
but I will give you a crown.

I can do the impossible,
no need to fear and dread.
I died on the cross for your sins,
and I came back from the dead."

"Walk with Me," Jesus says,
"down that winding road.
Take my yoke upon you, child,
and I will share the load.

I will help you bear the burden;
I will help you all the way.
I will walk beside you,
each and every day."

He Who Never Began

He who will never end,
is He who never began;
from everlasting to everlasting,
He is the Great I Am.

Who can stand up to the LORD of Hosts?
Who can fathom His ways?
Who can approach His Holy Throne,
and worship the Ancient of Days?

What right have we to call on Him?
What right have we to pray?
We who are evil and unholy of heart,
and wicked in every way.

But we are cleansed by the Lamb of God,
and rescued by the Son of Man;
and reconciled to Him who will never end,
to Him who never began.

The Calm in the Midst of the Strife

"Never," he says, "will I leave you;
never will I go away.
My promise is true no matter the trial,
I am with you every day."

"Come to Me when you need rest, come when
you're tired and troubled.
The cares of this world are too heavy for you,
with Me you can endure the struggle."

"Believe Me, My child, I know your pain,
and you do not walk alone.
But My ways are not yours and
yours are not Mine,
just trust me in all the unknown."

"Love me with all your mind and strength,
love me with all your heart.
I am Your Savior and I give you My word,
all hell can't tears us apart."

"I am the way, you know this is true;
I am the truth and the life.
I am your calm in the midst of the storm,
your peace in the midst of the strife."

In All Things

In all things He works, in all things He plans,
for all things we face, are all in His hands.

In all things great, in all things small,
in all things unknown, God arranges them all.

In all things, is what He says,
in all things, is what he means,
In all things he weaves
His plan and moves behind the scenes.

In all things no matter what,
in all things no matter where,
In all things no matter when,
we're in His providential care.

In all things we wait on Him,
in all things we rest,
In all things we trust in Him,
for His will is always the best.

Lay Your Hand Upon Me, Lord

Lay Your hand upon me,
Lord, with your loving touch today.
Gently guide me so I may know
Your true and holy way.

Lay Your hand upon my heart,
for oft' it does not beat,
with Your concern and tenderness
for those I chance to meet.

Lay Your hand upon my mind,
so we will think as one.
May I think those blessed thoughts
of Jesus Christ, Your Son.

Lay Your hand upon my tongue,
so it I can restrain.
May I speak those things which are sweet,
and from evil to refrain.

Lay Your hand upon my soul,
and help me to look up.
Soothe my spirit with Your peace
from Your overflowing cup.

Lay Your hand upon me, Lord,
with Your mercy and Your grace.
Firmly lead me by the hand
to behold Your smiling face.

In Remembrance of Me

"Do this" He said, "in remembrance of me,
remember my pain and death on the tree.
And remember my life,
my words and my love,
my mercy and grace which bled from above.

"Eat and drink" He said unto them,
and with His disciples he sang a hymn
of praise and thanks to Jehovah the Great,
as He prepared for the path He must take.

Jesus, the Lord, the only Son,
God's chosen King, the Anointed One,
upon the cross endured the rage
and defeated the evil prince of this age.

The body of Christ they placed in a cave,
to serve the Lord as a cold, dark grave.
Death tried in vain to keep in the Light,
but He broke free in His righteous might.

At the right hand of god forever to reign,
A reminder to souls never to feign.
He still says to those whom He set free
"Eat and drink in remembrance of me."

The Little Red Car

I was waiting at a red light. There was a car in front me with a woman at the wheel. It was a nice red car. We waited for the light to turn.

Then I noticed the license plate. I had never seen it before. I enjoy decoding personalized plates. Most ae easy, many are clever, some are difficult and a few are nasty. Anyway, this car's plate really grabbed my attention.

The light turned green and that nice red car with that plate turned left, which was good, because I was turning left, too. So I followed her up the hill. She got over into the right lane and 3/4s of the way up the hill turned on her right turned signal. I decided to turn right, too. If she stopped at a convenient place I wanted to ask her about the story behind her plate.

But then I consider the wisdom of a man driving a mini-van with the license plate GRANKZZ following around a woman in a nice red car. So, I abandoned my pursuit and drove across the street into the church parking lot.

Why did I follow that car? What was on that plate? EPH C 2.

EPH C 2 has to stand for Ephesians chapter 2, the most well-known Bible passage about GRACE. I wanted to ask if she had a grace story to tell.

If you see a red car with that plate, and you get a chance, ask her if it has to do with grace. I bet it does.

Even if it doesn't, it was a "God wink" to me. What a great message to see driving around town.

Marvelous are His Works.

Mysterious are His Ways.

Magnificent are His Words.

I Wonder

Several years ago I left Baltimore and headed to Romney, West Virginia with a brief detour to Gettysburg.

But I took another detour that morning, too.

I headed northeast on Rt. 40 for about twenty miles and turned onto Philadelphia Road.

A few miles later I turned left onto Calvary Road, then turned right onto Goat Hill road, went a few hundred yards and turned left onto Creswell Rd. I passed Creswell Christian Church on the left and then came to a small campus which once was the home of Eastern Christian College (ECC), and where Karen and I met.

The campus is now the home to other ministries. I drove around campus, stopped and walked around for a few minutes. I saw a friend from "the old days" who works with one of the ministries which has offices in Old Main.

I then drove into Bel Air. Much has changed, few things have not. I located one place that ECC students used to haunt: Friendly's.

I then proceeded to drive to I-95 south but I turned around and headed back to Friendly's, went in and ordered breakfast and had perhaps the best ice-tea I ever had in a restaurant. I got one to go, too. I then headed to Gettysburg.

It does us good from time to time to go back in time. The ministry of memory is a wonderful gift not to be taken for granted. But it is equally important not to live in the past.

Time does not stand still, will not stand still, for anyone. Time is doing just what God designed it to do and will one day give way to a timeless eternity.

I have often wondered when we move to the New Earth, will we be able to go "back in time" to see what the world was like when we were born, to see ourselves on the first day of school, to watch a little league game in which we played, to witness our baptism?

Perhaps we can watch the 20th Maine defend Little Round Top? Maybe we will be able to actually see God creating the heavens and the earth, watch the Ark float on the waters, stand on a ridge as David slays Goliath?

Will we be permitted to weep at the foot of the cross and witness the resurrection?

I do not know, but it is nice to consider.

Route 666

Interstate 81 has been part of my journey since 1978 when Karen and I moved to Knoxville TN to study at Johnson Bible College, uh, I mean Johnson University as it is now called.

I cannot tell you the number of times we have headed up and down that stretch of road, usually getting off at Winchester to go to Romney or going on up to Hagerstown to take 70 to Baltimore, Maryland.

A few weeks ago while traveling back to Wise, Virginia, I saw a sign that I had never noticed before. I have no doubt that it has been there forever and that I have passed over 100 times. It is a small sign, but rather close to the highway. It reads, "Hogback Rd."

Its name reminded me of the Beverly Hillbillies. Perhaps Jed drove a road with a similar name to get to the general store before striking Texas Tea. Anyway, that same sign contains another designation for Hogback Rd. which I found even more amusing: Rt. 666.

I can imagine someone asking, "So where do you live." And the reply: "I live out on Hogback Rd." "Hogback Rd? I don't believe I know where that is."

"Sure you do....you know, Route. 6.....6.....6."

If you lived on that road, which designation would you prefer? Well think on this:

On the New Earth, I can imagine a road named "Hogback" (well, maybe), but I just can't imagine a road with the designation "666."

But who knows, God has a tremendous sense of humor. Maybe that is where I will live.

Sometimes My Shirt Tickles Me

One day I walked into our EduCare Preschool Center while the kids were finishing lunch and getting ready for nap time, all, that is, but one little girl.

This little girl, with blonde hair and an infectious smile, was still sitting at the table enjoying her lunch. She looked up at me and smiled.

I smiled at her and then she something that she felt I needed to know. She said, "Sometimes my shirt tickles me."

Right out of the blue, that is what she said.

We were not talking about shirts or being ticked, or anything like that.

I laughed and said, "Sometimes your shirt tickles you?"

She smiled and nodded. I guess she felt that she needed to tell someone, and I was that someone.

There are times when we adults long for simpler times, when we had no cares, no issues; when we were kids and the biggest thing on our minds was what game to play at recess or playing sandlot baseball on Saturday morning.

Jesus often uses children as a model for discipleship, telling us that we need to change and become like little children, specifically pointing out the humility of children.

And one thing children do a lot is to innocently speak what they are thinking. Do you think that is what our Father wants from His children, to share with Him what we are thinking, even if it is something trivial?

Maybe it would bring joy to His heart to hear one of His kids say, "Sometimes my shirt tickles me."

Really?

So the other day I was heading down the hill into the Town of Wise and I had a few things on my mind. Things that puzzled me and I was wondering what God was up to. I said under my breath, "I wish I could figure Him out."

And almost immediately the thought hit me-

"Really? Really? Do I really wish I could figure God out? Really?"

Perhaps you have thought or said something like that, "I wish I could figure God out." But do we want to live under the providence of a God we can figure out? Do we want to be loved by a God we can comprehend?

Do we want to be saved by a God whose ways we understand and whose thoughts could fit into our tiny minds?

It is written in Isaiah 55:8,9, "For my thoughts are not your thoughts, neither your ways my ways," declares the LORD. "As the heavens are higher than the earth, so are my ways higher than your ways, and my thoughts than your thoughts."

Remember: We do not have to understand God in order to trust God. Marvelous are His words, mysterious arc His ways!

A Lesson from Cracker Barrel

You have heard it said, "Familiarity breeds contempt." I suppose it is true that prolonged association with a person may result in loss of respect for that person. And, of course, when others have prolonged association with us they may develop contempt for us.

I would hope, however, that putting into practice the love of Christ would be the antidote for "familiarity breeds contempt."

Something happened when Karen and I had to make a trip to Baltimore, MD. It is a place that I am somewhat familiar with. I find it uncomfortable. It is too big, too hurried, too crowded, to impolite and too flat.

While there we drove up to Bel Air. It was there in 1976 I met Karen. We both were students at good ol' Eastern Christian College.

We have visited the Bel Air many times since, and each time we found big changes. One change that surprised us was a closed Friendly's restaurant.

It was place where we students went many times. The building was run down and abandoned. But everywhere else there were signs of progress, so much so that I had difficulty finding my way out of Bel Air and back to Baltimore. New landmarks have a way of obstructing old landmarks. A sign of the times, I suppose.

Well, we decided to find somewhere else to have dinner. I knew that a Cracker Barrel was somewhere nearby. It was not there back in the 70s and we have never been to this particular one, but we have visited many Cracker Barrels at many locations over many years.

I finally found it and when we walked through the doors, something very welcoming happen: We stepped into a familiar place. And this happens no matter which Cracker Barrel you visit. They are all about 99% the same. And that is a good thing. No matter where you travel, no matter how far you are away from home, no matter how pleasant or ugly the surroundings, when you step into a Cracker Barrel, you find a familiar place.

Familiarity can be a good thing. It breeds a sense of place and belonging. It provides security and comfort. It produces peace and contentment. It reduces stress and anxiety. It is a respite from fast changing things.

We, who are in this world but not of this world, are blessed to find the Church. . . a familiar place.

It Made Me an Offer
I Couldn't Refuse

Several years ago I was in a local department store. I was at the counter when I heard, "Psst. Psst. Hey you. Come here."

I looked to my left and I saw a tie rack with at least 100 ties on it. And one of those ties wanted me to come over.

I walked over to see what it wanted and it said, "You have not seen a tie like me before, have you," and I had to admit I had not. It was a great Christmas tie, but I did not want to let it know that. It was trying to make a sale, so I played hard to get. I told it that I have a fairly large collection of Christmas ties. But it persisted, "I am on sale, ya know."

I said, "Yeah, how much?" and it showed me its original price of $20 and the sale price of $5. "$5...not bad," I said. Then it told me that since I am over 50 (the tie could tell) that I could get the senior discount.

So I took the tie off the rack, went to the counter and paid $4.20 and walked out with for a very cool Christmas tie, which I wore the following Sunday, and received many comments.

Not all stories have to make a point.

Bird Watching

One morning I looked out the window into one of the trees and I see a bird's nest with two Blue Jays and a few babies. I thought, "Mommy and Daddy Blue Jay and their kids getting ready to face the day.'

I was just about to look away when I see Mrs. Blue Jay help Mr. Blue Jay on with his overcoat (it was cold and rainy) and hand him his hat and brief case.

He kisses her and the kids, and flies away and disappears in the morning fog.

Mrs. Blue Jay tends to the kids and cleans up the kitchen. She then sits down at the table and sorts through her coupons and makes out her grocery list.

There is a look of concern on her face, as if the list is longer than what they could afford.

Well, I figure Mr. Blue Jay would be home sometime that evening and sure enough, I get home in time to see him return home.

He was tired and tattered; flying like Woodstock does in the Peanuts comic Strip. I can tell he had day at work.

He takes off his coat, kisses his wife, plays with the kids a while, and settles into his easy chair. After putting the kids to bed they sit in silence at the kitchen table.

He holds up a pink slip and just stares at her. He lost his job.

She holds up a stack of bills and begins to cry.

They hug each other until finally they turn out the lights and try to go to sleep. They have face life again in the morning.

Have you ever seen something like that? Of course not.

Jesus says, "Therefore I tell you, do not worry about your life, what you will eat or drink; or about your body, what you will wear. Is not life more important than food, and the body more important than clothes?

Look at the birds of the air; they do not sow or reap or store away in barns, and yet your heavenly Father feeds them. Are you not much more valuable than they?

Who of you by worrying can add a single hour to his life? And why do you worry about clothes?

See how the lilies of the field grow. They do not labor or spin. Yet I tell you that not even Solomon in all his splendor was dressed like one of these. If that is how God clothes the grass of the field, which is here today and tomorrow is thrown into the fire, will he not much more clothe you, O you of little faith?

So do not worry, saying, 'What shall we eat?' or 'What shall we drink?' or 'What shall we wear?'

For the pagans run after all these things, and your heavenly Father knows that you need them.

But seek first his kingdom and his righteousness, and all these things will be given to you as well. Therefore do not worry about tomorrow, for tomorrow will worry about itself. Each day has enough trouble of its own."

Matthew 6:25-34

Seek the Kingdom first. Just one day at a time, and God will take care of the rest. We have the Lord's word on that!

Bob's Gulf Station

As I have said before, I grew up in a great place. Johnny and Joyce Wells provided an ideal place to raise me and my four sisters, Diane, Lisa, Kelly and Wendy.

Our house was situated on top of a hill which provided for some fantastic sledding during the winter.

We would race down Second Street, cross over Central Ave, and then go up the other side of Second Street as far as possible, then turn around and repeat it. There were other outstanding sledding courses, too.

Behind my house was a hillside of woods with a babbling brook meandering through the valley floor which could be heard at night singing with the various wood creatures.

And we had cliffs to climb and occasionally fall from. I have a small scar on my left wrist as a result of one mishap. No broken bones, though!

Uptown was a place that provided some vivid memories, too.

One was Bob's Gulf Station, owned and operated by Bob, of course. He lived down the hill and up the street from me.

Bob's Gulf Station was a fascinating place for a young boy. It was a place where men would come in and "shoot the breeze," brag about how hard they worked and call each other colorful names.

It was also a place where hunters checked in their deer, which meant I saw a lot of dead deer tied to vehicles.

Chocolate milk, at five cents, was one of my favorite treats.

Bob's Gulf Station was also where I was introduced to an amazing concoction. You take an ice-cold bottle of Coke and pour a bag of salted peanuts in it.

I have not had one of those in a long, long time. I may, however, get a bottle of Coke (glass bottle, if possible) and a bag of salted peanuts for old times' sake.

Bob's Gulf Station is no more. The building houses a furniture store. The gas pumps and grease spots are long gone.

Every time I am in Romney I drive by. And remember.

Oh My, How Time Goes By

Growing up in my small town;
family, faith and friends around.
Memories of West Virginia hills;
colors of fall & winter chills.

Climbing cliffs and big old trees;
wading in the creek up to my knees.
Playing ball in a vacant lot;
raising my bat, calling my shot.

Oh my, how time goes by.
Oh my, how time goes by.
Oh how the years seem to fly.
My, oh my, how time goes by.

Knocking on doors, "trick or treat";
Thanksgiving meal, lots to eat.
Sunny days and snowy nights;
hanging up our Christmas lights.

Raking leaves and shoveling snow;
hated school, didn't want to go.
Going to church to praise the Lord;
Sunday School to learn God's Word.

Oh my, how time goes by.
Oh my, how time goes by.
Oh how the years seem to fly.
My, oh my, how time goes by.

Throwing knives in my back yard;
rigging bikes with baseball cards.
That World Series I can't forget;
I still don't like the New York Mets.

My four sisters picking on me;
my first job at the A& P.
Mom getting supper ready at five;
my dad teaching me to drive.

Oh my, how time goes by.
Oh my, how time goes by.
Oh how the years seem to fly.
My, oh my, how time goes by.

Saying "I do" to my lovely wife;
building a home, making a life.
One, two, three kids come along;
we all sing the "Sunshine" song.

They grow up and graduate;
leaving the nest, tough to take.
Now we're Granny and Granddad;
eight Grandkids, that's not bad.

Oh my, how time goes by.
Oh my, how time goes by.
Oh how the years seem to fly.
My, oh my, how time goes by.

I look in the mirror, blink my eyes;
I see a man I barely recognize.
I used to have a lot of hair;
now the top of my head is shiny and bare.

Aches and pains all over the place;
wrinkles appearing on my face.
Life is hard, but God is good;
giving me grace as only He could.

Oh my, how time goes by.
Oh my, how time goes by.
Oh how the years seem to fly.
My, oh my, how time goes by.

God declares the victory's won;
I'm heading home to see the Son.
When I go through Heaven's Door
time won't matter anymore.

Making an Impression

Nov. 4th, 2011 stopped at a convenience store on the way to Pikeville, got a few snacks, and got in line to pay.

The cashier was engaged in friendly banter with the people in line ahead of me, and even talking to someone behind me.

When I stepped up I greeted her but she said not a word. She rang up my items and did not even tell me how much I owed; I had to look to see.

I said, "Here you are" as I handed her the money. She gave me the change and I said "thank you." She said nothing.

As I drove off I thought about that encounter and wondered why it happened. Did I offend her in some way? Did I have BO? I don't think so?

What was it about me that caused her to give me the proverbial cold shoulder?

I wondered if it was what I wore. I was wearing a West Virginia hat. That had to be it.

Perhaps she was such a Kentucky fan that she could not bring herself to speak even a few courteous words to someone from a foreign land.

Later that day I shared what happened with someone more familiar with the ways of Southeastern Kentucky, and he said it was quite possible that was the reason.

Well, another, more probable, explanation came about the more I thought on it. Here it is: I was a stranger.

She had never seen me before. She did not know me. That little convenience store out in the middle of nowhere was a place "where everyone knows you name," and she did not know me and she had reservations. Does that sound implausible?

That place made an impression on me, a bad one. And that makes me think of how I interact with those I do not know.

We are the Church...
And We Win!

Members of the early Church were real people living in a real world.

- They confronted life-challenging issues, just like us.

- They were concerned about their economy, just like us.

- They had issues with their government, just like us.

- They were faced with all kinds of immorality, just like us.

- They had competing religious and philosophical ideas, just like us.

- They were aware of wars and rumors of wars, just like us.

- They faced natural disasters, unexpected tragedies, just like us.

- They were concerned about the safety of their children and grandchildren, just like us.

They were encouraged to remember the Good News of Jesus Christ. Christ is to be of supreme importance in you and in your family and in your Church. He is to have priority.

Let Him guide your life, shape your worldview, give you hope, inspire your confidence, calm your fears, encourage your hearts, influence your opinions, ideas, and plans.

The Church is not to sit in the corner wringing our hands with despair, intimidated by our culture, fretting about our fate, worried about this world as if it is our home.

Our home is secure. Our future is certain. Our inheritance is eternal. Our hope is steadfast. Our outlook is optimistic.

- Our destination has no political parties, no immoral policies, no abortion debates.

- No backroom deals, no bankrupt budgets, no sleazy scandals, no congressional investigations.

- No legal challenges, no court decisions, no news shows, no republican pundits, no democrat strategists, no libertarian advocates, no angry demonstrations, no hopeless issues and no helpless situations.

As someone put it: Our Leader, our Savior, our Lord, our Commander-in-Chief, our King is:

- perfectly righteous, personally involved, perpetually in charge, prolifically creative;

- powerfully endowed, permanently enthroned, preeminently worshipped;

- providentially successful and prevailingly triumphant.

The world is winding down. Time is speeding up. Jesus is coming back.

Come Lord Jesus. The grace of the Lord Jesus be with God's people. Amen.

Revelation 22:20

The Fringe of Fellowship

James Moore, in his book "The Top Ten List for Christians," tells the story of a young priest who was assigned to serve a Catholic Church in Colorado.

On his first Sunday he noticed from his study window a full parking lot, but when he walked into the sanctuary, he saw only 15-20 souls in the pews. The next Sunday the same thing happened. On the third Sunday he positioned himself where he could see people get out of their cars and enter the building.

Sure enough, a lot of people got out of their cars and entered the building, but most of them entered just far enough to dip a finger in the holy water and make the sign of the cross and then leave!

I choose the term "living on the fringe of fellowship," to describe the people in that story.

"Fringers" make up a sizeable demographic in Church culture.

- They try to stay within the circle, but far from the center.

- They want to be part of the circle, but only on the perimeter.

- They are Pluto orbiting our sun from an extreme distance, still part of the solar system but whose planetary status is debated.

- They attend their family reunion, but stay a hundred feet away, hearing only distant chatter and laughter, never venturing close enough to share hugs and smiles and to celebrate the joys and encourage the sorrows of their family.

- Never close enough to hear the latest news.

- Then, on the drive home, they gripe about the bad time they had and say they may not be back.

- It was not what they expected and not worth the effort.

The story told by Moore may amuse us and sadden us.

We may even mutter that we would never do anything like that. I wonder if it is possible that we come in just far enough to get a dose of "religion," just far enough hoping to clear our conscience, just far enough expecting that the kids will get a magic Bible lesson in Church that may make them behave in school.

"Just far enough" is another way of saying, "living on the fringe."

It is not right, and it does not work.

It Is On The Way!

One evening I was sitting in one of my favorite places in the world...my back deck. Sometimes I get some serious thinking done there. Sometimes.

Anyway, I was listening to the radio and I was getting disgusted at how our government seems to lack common sense and sound judgment

I have believed for a long time that our nation will not be conquered from without; rather, we will rot from within. Our weakened foundation will not hold indefinitely. We will crumble beneath the weight of a spirit of satanic stupidity.

And then, God spoke. He reminded me of something we dust off and bring out at Christmas. A promise to His people about His Son:

The government will be upon his shoulders.

Isaiah 9:6

Government itself is not sinful. The problem is that right now sinners are in government, and sinners are also among the governed.

"All have sinned" means just that: All. from 1600 Pennsylvania Ave. in Washington, DC to my house in Wise, Virginia.

And much of the time the sinners in government are <u>not</u> sinners saved by the grace of God through faith in Christ.

They do not confess Jesus as Lord. And since "the god of this world has blinded" their minds (II Cor. 4:4), their decisions and policies reflect their spiritual darkness.

Yes, our government, and every government in the world, is a testimony to the terrible choice that was made at an address somewhere in Eden.

But, the best is yet to come: A perfectly GOOD Government is on the way!

* * *

The kingdom of the world has become the kingdom of our Lord and of his Christ, and he will reign for ever and ever.

Revelation 11:15

Of the increase of HIS government and peace there will be no end."

Isaiah 9:7

God Smiled

We gathered at 8:00 in the morning; 200 souls gathered for a specific purpose. Two hundred elementary and middle school students, teachers and staff gathered for "Prayer at the Pole" day.

It was the coldest morning yet of the young autumn season, but we all circled up around the flagpole. It was something to behold, seeing so many children with their book bags standing next to each other with their teachers and staff getting ready to pray.

I was asked to participate. I saw this as an opportunity not only to pray with the students, but to teach them about prayer so I made 150 copies of "The Lord's Prayer" to be distributed to everyone.

When we mentioned that some would have to share, the little girl standing next to me said that someone else could have her copy, and then proceeded to whip out her own copy of The Lord's Prayer which she carries with her to school, along with her well-worn copy of the New Testament! You never know.

I took a few moments to discuss prayer and talked about how we can pray like Jesus at anytime and at any place, even at school.

I demonstrated to them how we can personalize "The Lord's Prayer" for ourselves and for family and friends.

And then we did what we gathered to do.

We prayed.

We all prayed.

We all prayed "The Lord's Prayer" out loud together, from the heart. It was a moving thing to hear so many voices in unison praising God. It made me think of the song we sing: "Take joy my King, in what you hear, may it be a sweet, sweet sound in your ears."

It was a good morning, and I believe God smiled.

Breakfast with Jesus

Seven disciples went fishing.

They had seen the Risen Lord on two other occasions. The first time was on the evening of the day of his resurrection and the second time was a week later.

These visits were made behind locked doors for the benefit of the disciples; to encourage them and to enable them to testify that they were eyewitnesses to his resurrection.

But, this appearance seems to be for a different reason, made so Jesus and his closest friends can spend some quality time together before Jesus ascends to the Father.

And this appearance is made, not in Jerusalem behind locked doors, but early one morning as the sun begins to shed its light on the Sea of Galilee.

Jesus prepares breakfast, hosts breakfast and serves breakfast, perhaps stirring memories within his disciples of the Passover Meal where Jesus served them by washing their feet.

Knowing Jesus and knowing the personalities of some of the disciples, and considering all they had just experienced, something like this may have taken place:

They are gathered around the fire. They are eating the fish and the bread. They are laughing and talking about the "good ol' days."

James says, "You know, I remember hearing the Baptist preach standing knee-deep in the Jordan and pointing at Jesus.

Do you remember what he said, John? Do you remember Peter? I remember.

He said, 'Behold, the Lamb of God who takes away the sin of the world.' I remember that as if it were yesterday."

Another says, "Lord, do you remember that time in the synagogue when You healed that lame man? Man, what a reaction from the people. They could not believe it!"

Another says, "I will never forget the day when You raised Lazarus. Un-be-lievable!"

Then they start ribbing each other. John says, "Hey Matthew, do you recall when we walked up to you and Jesus gave you 'the call?

You almost fell off your stool. I thought that the last man we needed was a tax collector. I still do!"

Matthew responds, "Well, at least I did not want to call down fire from heaven on that little village. You know, you and James really do have bad tempers. You better do something about that."

"What about old Nathanael," says James, "do you remember what he said, 'Can anything good come out of Nazareth?' Can anything good come out of Nazareth!? What were you thinking?"

Nathanael looks across the fire at Jesus, who is looking at him, and softly says, "I can't believe I said that."

Now things get a serious. Thomas, looking at the hands of Jesus just inches away, says, "I can't believe I said what I said, 'unless I see the marks, I will not believe.'"

Jesus reaches over and squeezes his knee. Thomas once again sees the marks.

Peter begins to weep. He cries, "I can't believe I did what I did. Three times." John puts his arm around him.

Someone mumbles, "Remember what Judas did? Do you remember what we all did when they came to arrest him? We all ran away. Only John had the guts to be near the cross."

Now there is silence, except for the sounds of sobbing.

Jesus, staring into the fire, slowly breaks off a piece of bread. He pauses, and then He grins, and with a twinkle in his eye, says, "Yeah, but do you remember...Sunday?"

He begins to laugh, and they all begin to laugh, for they know what happened on Sunday, and they know what He means, and they know they will never be the same again.

Nothing will ever be the same again.

Perhaps something like that happened during that breakfast by the sea. When things were the saddest, when the disciples were the gloomiest, when they had been taken captive by their shame and sorrow, when they recalled their sins, Jesus said, "Do you remember Sunday?"

Wouldn't you love to share a meal with Jesus? To be at a meal where Jesus is the host, and He invites you to sit down with Him? And to be with family and friends who also know Jesus and have been changed by Jesus?

And while you are there, you begin to talk and joke around, and remember times gone by.

You would say, "Do you remember the day I became a disciple?" Do you remember when I was baptized?"

Your buddy would reply, "Yes, I remember. I thought they were going to drown you because you had so many sins!"

And then you would think of the bad times; those times in which you were not faithful, times in which you betrayed and denied the Lord.

But Jesus, seeing your distress, would lay his hand on your shoulder and whisper, "Remember Sunday."

Yes, at the appointed time we will all be at the Great Supper Table with Jesus, but until then, we meet at His Table every Sunday, to remember, reflect, repent, receive and rejoice.

We sit down with Jesus.

He offers us the bread and He offers us the cup.

This is His meal,

He is the host.

And if we look carefully; if we look prayerfully; we might see Jesus standing by His table with a big smile on His face.

The Continuity of Communion

I cannot tell you how many times I have done it. have an approximate number, but not an exact number. Do you know how many times you have done it?

I confessed Jesus as Lord and was buried with Him in baptism in October, 1967 when I was 11 years old.

It happened almost fifty-four years ago at Romney Christian Church in Romney, West Virginia.

I figure that 2,800 (rounded down) Sundays have passed since my new birth in Christ and adoption by the Father.

2,800 Sundays on which Communion was celebrated.

Now, since September 1996 Norton Christian Church has had two Sunday morning services. Since I am at both services, I receive Communion at both services, so that brings the number of times I have participated in Communion since my baptism to approximately 4,100.

So I will round down to 4,000, allowing for times when I was not with the Church Family, for various reasons.

Every Sunday the Church participates in an act of grace where born again believers in Christ gather at the Lord's Table.

- In some churches it is called an ordinance, a term referring to a religious ceremony observed on a regular basis.

- In other churches it is known as a sacrament (Latin, meaning to consecrate, make holy). A sacrament is believed to be a physical means of spiritual grace. This is a term I have come to accept and appreciate.

- Another term that is not used much, although taken from Scripture, is The Eucharist, meaning Thanksgiving in Greek, and based on Paul words in I Corinthians 11. The Eucharist is a good term. Like sacrament, it even sounds appropriate.

- And, of course, the term Communion itself is from I Corinthians 10:16, translated "participation" in the NIV, from a word also translated as "fellowship."

There is one word that is often used by Christians that is not used in Scripture. It is symbol. I know we mean well when we use the word in reference to the Bread and the

Cup, and I do not want to wade into waters of legalism here, but the fact is Jesus does not use that word in reference to Communion.

Sometimes we feel the need to grope for words to explain something we have difficulty explaining, so somewhere back in time someone began using the word "symbol."

There is a mystery to this Meal, and that is a good thing. There have been theological debates for centuries about what Jesus meant when He said, "This is my body" and "This is my blood."

There are highly technical terms, such as Transubstantiation and Consubstantiation, that have been invented to try to wrap our minds around what Jesus means. Perhaps by comparison, symbol is not all that bad.

By grace we are saved through faith. God's grace poured out in the sacrificial death of Jesus for the sins of the world; for our sins. In Communion, we continue to receive grace upon grace.

I come to the Lord at His Table to remember, reflect, repent, receive, and rejoice.

I somehow, in some way, share, commune, participate, fellowship in the Body that was nailed to the Cross and in the Blood that was shed on the Cross.

Who can understand THAT? Not my puny mind.

Here is the thing. There is continuity in Communion. Much needed continuity. It is something I need.

A Tale of Two Churches

On Sunday June 24th, 2012, I worshipped with two different Churches separated by about ten miles.

Both Churches confess that Jesus is the Christ, the Son of the living God, who died for the sins of the world and was raised from the dead. Both Churches believe in the ministry of the Holy Spirit.

Both Churches believe in the authority of the Scriptures. Both Churches proclaim the reality of sin and the need for forgiveness. Both Churches want to see souls repent and believe the Good News.

Yet the two Churches differ in other areas, areas that have been the focus of years of Christian research which have produced volumes of data designed to assist Churches in numerical growth The pros and cons, and truths and errors of that research will also not be discussed here.

Here's the thing: "Church A" has two Morning Worship Hours. I attended the 9:00 a.m. service. "Church B" has one worship hour at 11:00.

"Church A" had three hundred total souls worshipping that day. "Church B" had five.

And Jesus was with both Churches.

Boga. Boga.

We are spoiled in many ways.

We also tend to do what is serious to us, no matter how hot or cold it is, and sometimes no matter how tired we are or how poorly we feel.

We do things such as walking Civil War battlefields in 90+ degree heat and a 99% humidity, sitting in sun-blistered bleachers while we watch little boys hit a ball with a stick, sink in sand while salt water laps at our feet, battle crowds at Pigeon Forge shops to buy stuff, etc.

Yet, we tend not to bring that same devotion to spiritual matters. As someone has said, we tend to worship our work, work at our play and play at our worship

American Christians can learn from our brothers and sisters in other countries.

I read about a practice that Christians in Uganda engage in as they prepare to worship and hear the Word of God.

As they sit in anticipation of worship, they chant, "Boga. Boga. Boga, Boga." In English that means, "Serious. Serious. Serious. Serious."

It gives me goose bumps to imagine such a scene.

Jesus is serious about worship. He says that true worship is spiritual and truthful and true worshippers are the kind of worshippers the father seeks (John 4:23,24).

Yes, Jesus is serious about worship. Worship is the highest expression of the human spirit.

It is, as one Christian puts it, "the highest corporate act of the Body of Christ." What an honor it is for us to come together for the purpose of praise, to join hearts, minds, and souls together in worship of God. Worship is a God-blessed way for us to grow in our walk with Him. And it is serious.

If we take God seriously, we will take worship seriously! "Boga. Boga!"

God Allows U-Turns

Karen and I have done a lot of traveling over the past many years, and there were times when I ended up being a little, shall I say, directionally challenged.

I remember one trip in December 2000. It was on a Sunday and I left after worship for Ft. Jackson, South Carolina. I had never been there before.

All went well until I reached the city limits of Columbia, and then something happened.

I followed the direction I got off the AAA Website, but either the directions were wrong or I misread them, but I ended up in downtown Columbia.

Now, after I realized that I was going in the wrong direction, I could have just stopped and sat in my pickup and said, "I am so sorry that I drove in the wrong direction. I am so sorry that I am where I am. I am so sorry that James will be left at Ft. Jackson over the holidays. I am so sorry that Karen will have to go on without me. I am sorry that the Church will never know what happened to me. I am sorry, sorry, sorry."

NO, I didn't do that. I stopped going in the wrong direction and started to go in the right direction.

The Greatest Question Ever Asked

Luke tells us that two angels appeared when the women went back to the tomb of Jesus early on that glorious first day of the week. And when the women arrived, they saw the stone rolled away and they saw these two men in clothes that gleamed like lightning.

The women were frightened and bowed down with their faces to the ground. And the angels announced the Resurrection to them.

But at first, they did not simply say, "He is not here. He has risen."

They asked what has to be, without a doubt, absolutely, hands down, the single greatest question every asked.

They asked, "Why do you seek the living among the dead?"

Luke 24:1-8

Now, we are not told how these two particular angels were assigned this privilege.

I imagined every angel in heaven volunteered. But God chose these two, and perhaps God left it up to them to choose the words to say to the women.

So, here is what happened in my imagination:

* * *

Angel #1, we will call Him Bob, says to angel #2, we will call him Jim, "Well, what shall we say?"

Jim says, "Well, whatever we say, it has to be big. I mean, really big. It is going to be written down, and people throughout human history will be reading about this. It has to be BIG."

Bob says, "Well, duhhh. I know that so what shall we say? It needs to be memorable. Clever. Witty. Yet very appropriate."

Then, suddenly, it hits him.

Bob says to Jim, "I got it!!! Here is what we will say: 'Why do you seek the living among the dead?"

Jim shouts, "That's brilliant. hat's awesome. That's inspired! That, then, is what we will say."

And the rest is history.

I Can Still Hear the Laughter

It was a moment that a few of us pastors still talk about. Only a few of us are left in the area, but we truly enjoy telling the story. It is part of the oral history of our Ministerial Association.

It has become a true urban legend.

It took place in the early 1990s. About a half-dozen area pastors met to plan the Annual Community Thanksgiving Service. We were pastors from different Churches, and we had different personalities. Most of us had a great sense of humor, and one was more serious and scholarly.

The serious pastor suggested that we include "The Great Prayer" in the Liturgy (Psalm 136). And the pastor selected to read that prayer was a good ol' boy with a noticeable country accent.

So, when he was assigned to pray "The Great Prayer," he responded in a slow way, "Well I don't know about a great prayer. How 'bout a perty good prayer?"

Everyone exploded in laughter.

Well, almost everyone.

A Poem of Praise

Let us praise the One Who sent the Son
to the place where the cattle fed;
to where only a humble manger was found
for the Son to lay His head.

Let us praise the One Who sent the Son
to the cross upon the hill;
to the cross where He offered up His life
and for our sins His blood to spill.

Let us praise the One Who sent the Son
and raised Him from the grave;
Who brought Him back
from the bonds of death,
and to Whom all power He gave.

Let us praise the One Who sent the Son
because of His great love;
Who will send Him back to earth again
to take us to His home above.

The Christmas Story as Recounted by the Little Theologians of EduCare Preschool

Once upon a time, an angel came to Mary and told her she would have a baby.

She <u>freaked out</u> but she said "yes." Mary was going to marry Joseph.

Joseph went to work and then went to bed. In his dream that night, the angel told him that Mary was going to have that baby and call him Jesus. Joseph said "ok."

So they got married and went to Bethlehem so they could pay the President a lot of money.

Then it was time for the baby, so they went to the hotel but it was full so they went to the barn.

Mary had her baby named Jesus. He was born in the manger that the cows ate hay out of. But they wrapped Jesus in a blanket before they put him on the hay.

Next, the angels sang and went "doo doo doo doo doo doo..." to tell the shepherd Jesus was born and they felt scared but the angels told them not to be.

So they said, "Let's go bye-bye and find Him." And they left their sheep to go to find baby Jesus.

Then the wise men came to bring presents to Jesus. They brought food, cows, necklaces, jewels and murph to Him.

So now we celebrate Christmas because it is Jesus' birthday.

And we get presents because Jesus got presents.

He came to earth to watch us because He loves us."

I love the way kids see things and say things.

The Fullness of Time

Jesus is standing on the Balcony of Heaven, overlooking the starry universe.

He looks down into space, past billions of galaxies, each containing billions of stars.

Deeper and deeper through the light years of beauty and splendor, until he finds the one called "The Milky Way."

He notices Halley's Comet streaking by and says, "Right on time."

He zeroes in on a small planet, the third from a certain start, a planet called "Earth." And there He sees a world of humanity, filled with sorrow and suffering.

He sees violence and bloodshed. He hears screams of pain and cries of despair, and prayers for deliverance.

He knows the condemnation Earth is under. The human race needs to be rescued.

Jesus scans the planet until He finds a small country in the Mediterranean Basin called Israel. In Israel there is a small village called Nazareth.

In Nazareth He sees a certain couple, a godly couple; hard working Joseph and his beloved Mary.

Jesus looks south and located another small town, Bethlehem. There is a stable there, where the beasts of the field are kept. He feels the cold, damp air. He smells the odors.

Jesus peers 33 years into the future and sees the city of Jerusalem, where His Father's House is located.

He looks just outside the city, just past the city wall, and sees a hill. A hill called "the Place of the Skull."

He sees a cross there. He stares at the cross. He cannot take His eyes off the cross. He sees nothing but the cross.

His silent stare is broken by the voice of His Father.

"Son," God says.

"Yes, Father," Jesus says.

"It is time."

"Yes Father."

He Came into the World

He came into the world,
while the world went on its way;
slipping into a tiny town,
His throne a bed of hay.

The unwanted and the lonely,
the powerless of the earth,
were blessed to hear the news,
and were invited to His birth.

They hurried to that sacred place,
to see Messiah begin,
His prophetic journey to the cross,
to rescue them from sin.

From the manger to the cross,
and every step between,
The Savior of the human race
was by sinners heard and seen

The Word of God became flesh
and issued the invitation,
to take up a cross and follow Him,
and participate in salvation.

He came into the world,
at Christmas we remember most,
that peaceful scene in Bethlehem,
announced by heavenly host.

God still visits the poor in spirit,
the humble and the meek;
those whose hearts are open,
the Son of God to see.

He came into the world,
while the world when on its way;
and a time known only by god,
He's coming back one day.

And when He makes His glorious return,
He will give a mighty shout,
And the world will know who He is, f
or He'll leave no room for doubt.

'Twas The Week Before Christmas
(The Great Christmas Blizzard of 2009)

'Twas a week before Christmas
in our Hallmark House,
two creatures were stirring,
we had killed the mouse.
Sitting by the fire watching
the snow come down,
we knew it would be
a White Christmas in Town.

Then a flicker, then two,
and the power went out,
this is going to be bad—
we had little doubt.
Through five dark nights
and long dreary days,
we kept hoping electricity
would soon come our way.

We took all the food from
out of the fridge
and buried it under
a deep snow ridge.
We scrounged up some batteries
for our radio,
and listened to hear
how much it would snow.

We looked out the windows
throughout the night,
hoping to see

a small glimmer of light.
Candles, flashlights
and extra blankets, too,
doing what we had
to make it through.

We waited and waited
for power to restore,
Then we waited and waited
and waited some more.
Some aches and pains
and an occasional cough,
but we knew that others
were much worse off.

Looking back on the week
leading to Christmas Day,
We must pay attention
to what God has to say.
We know that life
indeed takes a toll,
but the best work of Christmas
is inside the soul.

In the events of life God
will whisper and shout,
when it comes to His Light—
the Dark can't put it out.
So remember these truths
and never lose sight
Merry Christmas to all,
and to all a good night.

A Reminder That I Was A Grandad

As if having grandkids is not enough to remind me I am getting older, there are always other reminders. Case in point: Playing ball with Granddaughter Megan.

Megan is our oldest grandchild. She has grown into a remarkable young woman. But that was not always the case, for she is responsible for one of the first big reminders that time was catching up with me.

Karen and I were visiting the grandkids in Illinois. Megan was 11 at the time.

We were playing wiffle ball in the back yard, and because she was so fast (and I was not), I had difficulty getting her out. So I had to come up with a solution to the problem, and I did. Grandkids will force you to improvise and adapt rather quickly.

I made up a rule where all I had to do was to throw the ball at her, hit her and she would be out. I know that sounds bad, but it had to be done, I was getting really tired really fast. And besides, it was a wiffle ball.

Yes, Megan reminded me, unintentionally, that I was official a granddad.

But I would not have it any other way.

A Story

Rachel wakes up one morning and begins the day like most other days. Her husband, John, was already off to work. They have a little boy and a little girl.

She gets them up, feeds them, and rattles off a list of chores. She promises they can spend the day with their aunt and cousins next door. They rush their chores and she sends them off. Now, she is all alone, she sits down to catch her breath.

She is a good woman, respected by her family and friends. A good citizen. She worships with God's people on a regular basis. But she has her faults; she has her sins, one sin that she cannot seem to overcome. She knows it is a sin.

It began about two months ago, when she met David. He seemed to have appeared out of nowhere, while she was shopping at the local vegetable stand.

They chatted and she thought that was it, but she kept running into him about every other day or so, and they would talk some more, and he would compliment her.

It had gotten to the point where she hoped their paths would cross. Even though she knew that they had became too friendly. Then eventually their friendship turned to adultery.

So she sits in her kitchen wondering about herself, her life, her husband and kids and about him.

They had met three times, and he wants to meet again, today, at noon and she does not know what to do.

Part of her screams "NO" and part of her whispers "yes."

"Yes" wins.

* * *

She heads for the door and stops. She takes a long look around her little home. She sees a toy in the corner her son failed to put up. She goes over and puts it in the toy box her husband made last year.

She rubs the smooth surface and stares into space, and then she heads for the door again, and out she goes.

She slowly walks to where they meet. As she turns a corner she bumps into an old friend.

They exchange the latest about their kids, and she laughs nervously when her friend kids her about looking as if she is up to something.

As she says good-by, her friend says, "Tell that good lookin' husband of yours I said 'hi.'"

* * *

On she goes, until she comes to a side street. She quickly slips down the alley, through a rotting door and into the arms of her lover, telling herself that this is really the last time.

Ten minutes pass and then suddenly, three men burst through the door. She screams and covers herself.

David gets up and runs away. She screams his name, but he is long gone, and she is left alone.

The men grab her and pull her from the bed, yelling obscenities at her. She struggles, but their grip tightens, fingers digging into her arms.

They drag her from the room, and down the street. She stumbles. They yank her up. She stumbles again.

What is happening, she wonders. Who are these men and what are they going to do?

She looks over to the right and she sees her friend she had just talked with. Their eyes meet. She hangs her head, her hair covers her face.

By now, a crowd is forming and following.

Things are very noisy. She sees the market where she first met David. She sees her house off in the distance.

She sees, getting larger with each step, a very familiar place, and now she knows where they are taking her.

They pull her up the great steps and they enter the Temple Courts. There are many people there and huddled around someone.

Her captors yell, "Make way. Make way. We want to see the Nazarene. Make way!"

And they push through the crowd and throw her to the ground at the feet of Jesus.

They yank her up and make her stand in humiliation. She is shaking and bleeding.

Jesus looks at her. She looks at him and immediately looks away, a spectacle of sin and shame, and she has no excuse.

The men level their accusations, charges of adultery.

"Teacher, this woman was caught in the act of adultery. In the Law Moses commanded us to stone such women. Now what do you say?"

And they wait to hear. Someone begins to chant, and others join, "Stone her, stone her, stone her!" And she sees several men with stones already in their hands ready to throw.

The crowd has become a mob.

* * *

Her accusers motion for them to be quiet as they wait to hear what Jesus says; as she waits to see what Jesus does.

He looks at her, then at her accusers, and then at the crowd, and He bends down and writes on the ground.

And they strain to see what he writes. People begin whispering, "What is he writing, can you see?"

A young man says, "Wait, wait, I see it. He is writing, 'You shall not commit adultery.'" Many shout their approval at what He writes.

Then Jesus writes a list of other sins, too. "Lust, envy, pride, greed. Hypocrisy."

He knows that this woman's accusers are guilty of a multitude of sins themselves, and they know it too.

But they try to re-focus attention on the woman, and Jesus stands up with a rock in his hand and shouts, "If any one of you is without sin, let him be the first to throw a stone at her."

And they are taken aback at his aggressive behavior and bold words.

Nobody steps forward to take the stone. Jesus throws it to the ground, again stoops down and writes on the ground.

"What is he writing now?" someone asks.

An old man with a long beard smiles approvingly and says softly, "He is writing names."

And the old man walks away.

And after a few tense moments, one at a time her accusers leave. Now, they are alone.

Unsure of what to expect, she braces herself as Jesus stands up and faces her. She hesitates, and then slowly looks into his eyes.

He stares at her, as if looking into her soul. She feels it. He is about to speak, she feels that, too.

He says, in a gentle tone: "Woman, where are they? Has no one condemned you?"

Unsure of what is now happening, she summons what little strength she has to dare a reply. She meekly says, "No one, sir."

And then she hears Him say, "Then neither do I condemn you. Go now and leave your life of sin."

And when she hears these words, her weeping stops for a moment, a moment of disbelief, and then she sheds tears of joy.

* * *

Forgiven, as if she had never met David, as if she had never committed adultery, as if she had never broken her vows to God and to her husband.

She turns to leave, she takes another look into those eyes of Jesus. And Jesus smiles.

And she walks home, hoping her husband will be just as forgiving.

You know that story, don't you?

Of course you do. It is a story of sheer unadulterated, undeserved grace from the One who is full of grace; from whom we receive "grace upon grace," time and again.

My Sheep is Safe!

Karen and I had an opportunity to babysit our grandson Jackson and granddaughter Angela. Their and daddy and mommy (John and Emily,) lived in Kingsport, TN, at the time, about an hour away. Daddy and mommy had some business to take care of where we live, so it worked out well for us to spend some time with them.

Jackson brought with him one of his favorite toys, although it was much more than a toy to him. It was a little stuffed sheep, which he carried with him all the time.

And it so happened that when mommy and daddy got home that night that little stuffed sheep was nowhere to be found. It had run away so they called us and we looked around and we found it.

I said we would take good care of it until we saw each other again. All was right with the world, or so we thought.

That night Jackson had a terrible time going to sleep. He missed his sheep. He wanted his sheep. He needed his sheep.

So, Granddad to the rescue!

(Cue heroic action film music)

The next morning, I made a special trip down to Kingsport and personally delivered that special sheep.

When I walked into the house and held the sheep up, Jackson exclaimed, "My sheep is back. My sheep is safe."

He took it and hugged it and for him, all was right with the world.

His reaction made the trip all worthwhile.

Tough as Nails

It was the first time Angela and big brother Jackson spent the night with us. Jackson was almost six and Angela was three-and-a-half.

We had them for several days. We put them both on our pull-out couch and they got along great, often watching TV or playing with their books. When it was time to go to sleep, they went to sleep.

But something happened one day.

Jackson came into the family room with blood on his face. We did not hear anything unusual. Nothing crashed. No thud. No weeping and wailing.

When asked what happened, Jackson said he fell from off the bed. I said, "We told you should not jump up and down on the bed."

We cleaned him up and he was fine. In the course of time, Karen and I noticed something about Angela. Angela, a sweet, pretty little girl with beautiful hair, liked to beat up Jackson.

She would jump on him and wrestle him and pound on him, and Jackson, who could have easily stopped her, was a good sport and let her have her way.

So that got us thinking about the bloody nose.

I interrogated them, and finally got enough evidence to determine what happened. Jackson did not fall off the bed; Angela shoved him off the bed!

Now, I would like to think it was an accident, but I think the evidence may say otherwise!

Jackson better watch his back from now on.

A Breakthrough

Haley is our youngest grandchild, just 13-months-old as of this writing; the daughter of John and Emily Wells.

She is a beautiful little girl and big beautiful eyes, and an incredible set of lungs.

Now one thing about Haley is that she is a mommy's girl and a daddy's girl more so than her siblings, and during family get-to-gathers she would cry and scream if I held her, and the longer I held her the worse it got.

So, when asked to keep Haley and Jackson while mommy took Angela to speech therapy,

I was a little apprehensive. Jackson had been with us several times, but it would be the first time Haley would be with us without mommy and daddy.

When the day came Karen and I decided to divide and conquer.

She played with Jackson and I would focus on Haley. Even though I am a veteran granddad with plenty of experience under my belt, I was not sure how this would turn out.

But, we had a breakthrough.

Something happened and she got along with me with no problem.

What happened?

Well, I think it has to do with something I have had a lot of practice with rocking kids and grandkids.

There is something about a rocking chair and granddad's lap.

I rocked Haley, sung "You Are My Sunshine," and played with a new toy with her, a toy Granny picked up for her for that occasion.

We rocked and sang and played until mommy and daddy returned to pick her up and things changed (a little) that day.

It was like Haley said, "I trust you. . . for now."

A Note on a Tree

One Tuesday evening I arrived at the studio to at five-thirty to prepare for "Grace Notes," my six o'clock radio show.

Parked in front of the station, I was thinking about the upcoming show when I noticed something attached to one of the trees that line the Park Avenue sidewalk in Norton.

It was a post-it note.

I had never seen a post-it note on a tree before so I looked up and down the street at the other trees, but none had a post-it note stuck to it. Just the one I had parked beside.

So I went and looked at the note. It had a hand-written message on it. I wondered who wrote it and why they posted it on this tree right in front of the Radio Station. And why did only this tree have a note?

I leaned forward, remove my glasses and read the note. It was from the Bible. I recognized the quote from the Parable of The Weeds in Matthew 13.

Just two verses from that Parable:

"No," he answered them, "because while you are pulling the weeds, you may root up the wheat with them. Let both grow together until the harvest.

At that time I will tell the harvesters: First collect the weeds and tie them in bundles to be burned; then gather the wheat and bring it into my barn." (Matthew 13:29,30)

Of all the verses in the Bible, why these two verses? Why not John 3:16?   Psalm 23:1? Romans 8:28? Proverbs 3:5,6? Hebrews 11:1? Or even Revelation 22:20?

Why verses from a Parable about what will happen at the end of the age? Who wrote the note and who was the intended reader or readers?

Well, I have a habit of over-analyzing, but I decided not to over-analyze this note too much. I decided that perhaps that message was for anyone and everyone who walked up and down Park Avenue, including me.

Perhaps it was for anyone and everyone who took a minute to stop and read it. Maybe it was seed scattered upon the ground, to appeal to another Parable.

Well, this I do know: It was a much-needed reminder that God will settle things, in His own time and in His own way.

The wicked will be punished, and the righteous will be rewarded.

I told this story on the radio that night. Who knows? Maybe that is why that note was put there in the first place?

I drove down Park Ave the next day and the note was still there, for someone else to see, stop, and read, and be blessed.

So, put down this book and get your Bible and read the whole Parable of the Weeds in Matthew 13:24-30.

Keep that Parable in your heart.

Ponder that Parable often. And when you are saddened by the wickedness of the world, when you are sick and tired and cannot wait to go home, when you wonder why God is taking so long, let Jesus encourage you.

He knows what He is doing!

And if you ever see a note attached to a tree, take a minute and read it. Maybe it is a message you need to read, a truth you need to ponder, or a story you need to share.

***

Maybe it is something you need to think about.

About the Author

Jim Wells was raised in Romney, WV and in the Romney Christian Church. He is the son of Johnny and Joyce Wells, and the only brother to four younger sisters, Diane, Lisa, Kelly and Wendy.

He graduated from Hampshire High School in 1974, and studied at Potomac State College, Eastern Christian College, Johnson University (BA, MA) and Emmanuel Christian Seminary. He has held ministries in Wardnesville, WV, Maryville, TN and Nitro, WV.

Jim has served as pastor of Norton Christian Church, Norton VA since 1984, and hosts two radio ministries, "Bright Spots" and "GraceNotes." He co-edited and co-authored *Retreat of the Soul: Reflections on the Contemplative Life by the Bardstown Brothers*.

Jim married his college sweetheart, Karen Denise Ward, of Baltimore, MD. They have three children, Katie Estep (Mitch), John (Emily) Wells and James; and eight grandchildren, Megan, Elijah, Mollie, Lucas and Caleb Estep, and Jackson, Angela and Haley Wells.

Jim and Karen are owned by a low-down, good for nothing, rotten dirty dog named Gracie, who cannot be trusted.

Books By This Author

Retreat of the Soul chronicles the spiritual pilgrimage of a group of ministers from a variety of theological traditions as they contemplate the role of prayer in their lives. Their journey parallels their annual retreat to the Abbey of Gethsemani near Bardstown, Kentucky.

This collection of writings invites you to share in their spiritual journey of the soul.

Something to Think About

This collection of writings presents a positive Christian message, offers encouragement to those who may be discouraged, and illustrates Biblical Truths in a way that are entertaining, often humorous, and always thought-provoking.

Index of Bible Verses

Acts 2:38,39	13
Acts 4:12	59
Colossians 3:1-3	47
Daniel 2:20,21	39
Daniel 4:34, 35	39
Ecclesiastes 3:1-4	15
Ephesians 1:3, 4	62
Ephesians 1:11	81
Ephesians 2:8, 9	37
Ephesians 4:1,2	67
Ephesians 6:10, 11	44
Exodus 14:21, 22	49
Galatians 6:5	68
Galatians 6:10	53
Genesis 3:1-5	55
Hebrews 10: 24,25	5
Hebrews 11:1, 2	64
Hebrews 11:3	65
Hebrews 11:6	38
Hebrews 12:2	80
I Corinthians 2:9	26, 40
I Corinthians 12:4-7	50
I Corinthians 12:18	36
I Corinthians 12:27	63
I Corinthians 13:1-8	8
I Corinthians 13:4	8, 46
I Corinthians 15:3	79
I Corinthians 15:14	79
I John 1:15-17	69
I John 3:16	76
I Peter 1:15	75
I Peter 1:18, 19	51
I Peter 2:9	58

I Peter 5:8, 9	44
I Thessalonians 4:16-18	77
I Timothy 1:15	25
I Timothy 3:14, 15	63
II Corinthians 5:7	70, 84
II Corinthians 5:7,8	70
II Corinthians 12:7-10	31
Isaiah 9:6	176
Isaiah 9:7	177
Isaiah 30:15	52
Isaiah 46:4	41
James 1:2, 3	31, 64
James 4:13-25	9
John 1:14	82
John 3:16	13, 76
John 3:16-18	13
John 3:3	25
John 12:25	69
John 14:1-3	27
John 14:3	27, 67
John 15:4, 5, NKJV	73
John 16:33	30
Joshua 24:15	61
Luke 5:16	52
Luke 2:10, 11	83
Luke 24:1-8	192
Mark 15:16	48
Matthew 1:21	59
Matthew 5:13-16	21, 33
Matthew 5:43-45	19
Matthew 6:24	61
Matthew 6:25-34	163
Matthew 6:3	20
Matthew 7:12	19
Matthew 7:5	68
Matthew 7:24-27	29

Matthew 18:3-5	11
Matthew 19:14	43
Matthew 24:36	74
Matthew 24:44	74
Matthew 25:13	74
Nehemiah 8:10	33
Proverbs 3:5,6	9, 84
Proverbs 14:12	25
Proverbs 15:1	56
Proverbs 16:9	9
Proverbs 17:6	45
Proverbs 17:22	15
Psalm 1	10
Psalm 23:1-3	52
Psalm 23:6	67
Psalm 25:9, 10	71
Psalm 46:10	23
Psalm 51:10-12	35
Psalm 62:2	57
Psalm 111:1	22
Psalm 119:11	29
Psalm 12:8	24
Psalm 122:1	22
Psalm 126:2,3	15
Psalm 18:2	57
Revelation 11:15	177
Revelation 22:20	173
Romans 3:23	17, 25
Romans 3:23-25	17
Romans 5:8	17
Romans 8:28	38
Romans 12:17-19, 21	19

www.ingramcontent.com/pod-product-compliance
Lightning Source LLC
Chambersburg PA
CBHW070849050426
42453CB00012B/2095